John and Pat Underwood

# walk & eat
## around NICE

# CONTENTS

This pocket guide is designed for short break walking holidays based on Nice, using public transport (or a car, if you prefer). The city is easily and inexpensively reached by several budget airlines, and the climate makes for brilliant walking and excursions all year round.

Hop on a plane or a train for a long weekend or a week. You have in your hand enough walks, excursions, restaurants and recipes to last almost two weeks — so you can pick and choose the most appealing. The highlights at a glance:

- 12 varied day walks, each with topographical map
- 2 fairly long excursions — one by train, one by bus, with walks from each
- recommended restaurants and hotels
- recipes to make at your self-catering base or back home
- special section with hints on wheat-, gluten- and dairy-free eating and cooking in the south of France

# INTRO

# THE WALKS

The walks range from almost flat coastal rambles a 15-minute bus ride from the city to 'balcony' routes high above the famed Riviera and mountain circuits. The book is specifically designed for visitors using public transport. If you've only a long weekend, you may not want to spend time filling in forms to hire a car. Of course, if you *do* want to hire a car, you will have many more options in the hinterland. Our wider-ranging book, *Landscapes of Eastern Provence* (see www.sunflowerbooks.co.uk), would take you from the Italian border to the Rhône via 11 car tours and 36 walks.

But rest assured that you do not need your own wheels to cut a large swathe through the 'Pays niçois'. Almost all the walks in this book are easily reached by bus or train, and getting there is half the fun. Sightsee while someone else does the driving. It's amazing how much ground you can cover in just a week.

# THE EXCURSIONS

Two long trips are outlined. First is the wonderful rail journey on the 'Train des Pignes', a narrow-gauge railway built between 1890 and 1912. It begins right in the city centre, running on 'tram' lines, then spans 150km on its journey into the mountains. The scenery is awe-inspiring. The train is an ideal way to reach walks out of town.

The second excursion is by local bus up the Var Valley and then via the red-rock Cians Gorges, up to ski resort country, where you can take an idyllic circular walk.

## THE RESTAURANTS

There are restaurants and hotels at the start or end of many of the walks, most of which we mention. But many of them close out of season — just when the walking is at its best! Unless we know that a restaurant will welcome you all year round, we suggest that you return to Nice for dinner — perhaps making a local recipe yourself. *No restaurant has paid, in cash or in kind, to be included in this guide.*

A few of our recommended restaurants are at hotels where you might like to spend the night, especially if you want to have dinner there and there is no late public transport back to base.

## THE RECIPES

Most of our recommended restaurants were happy to share with us the *ingredients* used in their recipes, but the actual preparation remains their 'secret' (in truth, they are simply not written down, but just passed on from cook to cook over the years). So you can rest assured that we have cooked *all* of these recipes ourselves, to make sure they 'work'!

What we cannot guarantee, of course, is that they will taste as good back home as they did in France! So many factors come into play to make food taste better when you are on holiday — from the intangibles (the atmosphere and the sense of relaxation after a day's good walking) to the tangibles (hardness of the water, quality of the fresh market produce you can seek out when not pressed for time). So if you are in self-catering, why not try some of these recipes while you're in Nice?

We've made most of these dishes on the simple kind of cooker usually found in self-catering (two rings and a decent oven) — or on a barbecue. Many of them are casserole-style, not only easily managed with limited cooking facilities, *but* also virtually impossible to overcook, and there is hardly any washing-up! What's more, they always taste better when reheated after a few days. And good news for anyone suffering food intolerances: all of the recipes can be **gluten- and dairy-free** (see page 138).

# PLANNING YOUR VISIT
## When to go

The simple answer is — anytime outside mid-June to mid-September, when it's usually swelteringly hot, crowded to overflowing, and prices are at their highest. Moreover, trails in areas prone to forest fires (like the Esterel, Walk 5) are closed to visitors in summer, when the fire risk is very high.

New Year's Day lunch on the beach at Nice

We walk from Nice in all other months. Naturally late September and October are ideal for the mild temperatures and the autumnal colours in the hinterland. One has to take a chance with autumnal rains in October and November, but you can still expect temperatures in the 60s (17-20°C).

We often go at Christmas/New Year, to enjoy the festivities

and the clear winter skies. If you think it may be too cold, remember that New Year's Day lunch on the beach is a long-standing tradition in Nice!

February ushers in carnival, mimosa festivals, and more good walking — it's virtually spring. Plan on some rainy days in March and April, but rainy spells don't usually last very long. And at least when it rains in Nice, there's plenty to do indoors (apart from trying new recipes).

May and early June, with wild flowers galore, are simply glorious, as you would expect.

## Where to stay

Of course there is a wide choice of hotels of all grades all along the coastal strip from Cannes to Menton. But the *best* public transport base is Nice centre.

Rather than an hotel, consider staying in private accommodation or one of the apart-hotels in the city. We cooked most of our recipes at an apart-hotel. To find an apartment, either go to airbnb.fr or just search 'apartments in Nice France'; Google, for instance, will come up with hundreds of sites, including many privately-owned second homes.

## What to take

Remembering that this is to be a carefree week or weekend, pack simply! You don't have to 'dress' for dinner in Nice, no matter how elegant the restaurant.

We manage with a rucksack each, by wearing our walking boots on the flight. Apart-hotels have inexpensive laundry facilities (and there are also many laundries and launderettes in town), so you needn't take a lot of clothing either.

No special equipment is needed for any of the walks, but proper **walking boots** are preferable to any other footwear. Most walks in the Nice hinterland cross very stony terrain at some stage, and

The big wheel is a feature of festival time in Nice.

good ankle support is essential. In wet weather you will also be glad of the waterproofing. A **sunhat** and high-protection **suncream** are equally important; there is a real risk of sunstroke on some walks (especially in May/June). Each member of the party should carry a **small rucksack**, so that the chore of lugging the essentials is shared. *All year round* it is advisable to carry a **first-aid kit**, **whistle**, **smartphone** (the emergency number throughout Europe is 112), **torch**, **spare socks** and **bootlaces**, and some **warm clothing** (the *mistral* can blow up suddenly, with temperatures dropping up to 10°C/20°F!). A **long-sleeved shirt** and **long trousers** should be worn or carried, for sun protection and for making your way through the prickly plants of the *maquis*. Depending on the season, you may also need a **windcheat**, **lightweight rainwear**, **woollies** and **gloves** — or **swimming things**. Don't forget a **UK-to-Continental plug adaptor** and **battery chargers**. A **Swiss Army knife** is always handy, but of course cannot be packed in hand luggage! Although mineral water is sold everywhere in half-litre bottles, you may prefer to cut down on plastic usage by taking your own water container. *It is imperative that each walker carries at least a half-litre of water — a full litre or more in hot weather.*

## Planning your walks

The walks are specifically designed for access by the excellent **local transport** network … so that you can enjoy some wine with lunch! But if you *do* want to hire a **car**, and the route is linear, you can usually leave your car at the end of the walk and take a bus to the start.

The walks have been **graded** for the deskbound person who nevertheless keeps reasonably fit. Our timings average 4km per hour on the flat, plus 20 minutes for every 100m/300ft of ascent. None of the walks ascends more than about 500m/1650ft, although there are one or two steep descents. *Do* check your timings against ours on a short walk before tackling one of the longer hikes. Remember that these are *neat walking times*; increase the overall time by *at least* 50 percent, to allow for any breaks and nature-watching.

**Safety** depends in great part on *knowing what to expect and being properly equipped*. For this reason we urge you to read through the *whole* walk description at your leisure *before* setting out, so that you have a mental picture of each stage of the route and the landmarks. On *most* of our walks you will encounter other people — an advantage if you get into difficulty. Nevertheless, we advise you **never** to walk alone.

The **maps** in this book, adapted from IGN 1:25,000 maps, have been reproduced at a scale of 1:35,000 or larger. The relevant map numbers, should you wish to go further afield, are shown in the 'logistics' panel facing each walk introduction. All IGN 'Top 25' maps show local and long-distance walks.

Free **GPS track** downloads are available for all the walks in this book: see the *Walk & eat around Nice* page on the Sunflower website. *Even if you don't use GPS* on the ground, you could use the track downloads to preview the walks in advance.

Of the dozens of reasons why walking from Nice is such a joy, a particularly strong point is the superb **waymarking** and **signposting** carried out by the governing bodies of the Alpes Maritimes and Alpes de Haute Provence.

Basically you will encounter three types of waymarking:

**PR (Petite Randonnée)**: short walks, waymarked in yellow;

**GR (Grande Randonnée)**: long-distance routes, waymarked red and white;

**GRP (Grande Randonnée du Pays)**: a recently developed network of trails of varying lengths, designed to acquaint walkers with a particular region, waymarked red/yellow.

At the top of each walk we mention the waymarking colours *at time of writing*. Do, however, note these waymarking features, common to both PR and GR routes:

— A *flash* (stripe of paint) or *dot* indicates 'Route continues this way'. (The GR uses *two separate* flashes, red and white, and

this must *never* be confused with a red flash on a white paint ground, which is local boundary marking, *not* waymarking.)
— A right- or left-angled flash (or an arrow) means 'Change of direction' ( ⌐ indicates a right turn, ⌐ a left turn).
— An **X** means 'Wrong way'.

## Verifying timetables in advance

While transport details are given in the 'logistics' panel at the start of each walk, remember that these timetables were *correct at time of writing*. The *very best* way to verify departures and returns is at the information desk at the relevant stations after you arrive. But if you want to plan some walks in advance, you can verify timetables online before you travel.

**Trains** are operated by TER (Transports Express Régional), part of the SNCF (Société Nationale des Chemins de Fer). Their website (**www.sncf.com/en**) comes up with a 'Plan my journey' option at the start, followed by more options including rail passes. But to see timetables at a glance, we find it easier to use **www.thetrainline.com**!

SNCF offers a 'Summer Day Pass' costing just 16 €, which allows you to hop-on, hop-off any TER coastal train from Menton (Walk 8) to Théoule (Walk 5) *plus* discounted entry to various tourist attractions; sadly, this is only available from 1 June to 30 September. By far a better bet, and available all year round, is the 'Carte ZOU Hebdo', a hop-on, hop-off *weekly* pass for the coastal trains costing just 35 €! You can buy these passes online or at the ZOU office (near the left luggage) in the railway station — or at an SNCF counter if the ZOU office is closed.

Golden-hued 18th-century façades grace Old Nice.

Timetables for the delightful, privately-owned **Train de Pignes**, operated by the Chemins de Fer de Provence (Excursion 1, Walks 9 and 10), *cannot* be accessed at sncf.com. To see their timetables, go to **www.trainprovence.com**. Click on 'Nice > Digne', then on 'Times and Fares', where you can download a PDF — as well as brief descriptions of a few other walks accessible from the train.

**Intercity buses** are operated by TAM (Transports Alpes-Maritimes). The most useful website for their timetables, fares and the various passes is **www.sudmobilite.fr**. Just click on the English version and away you go — it's very easy to use.

The sudmobilite.fr website also covers all buses out of **Menton**, which are run by a company called Zest (currently with no web presence except on Facebook). You will want to use Zest buses for Walk 7 (bus 10 from Menton to Ste-Agnès and bus 6 back from Castellar or bus 15 back from Monti). This website will also be especially helpful to anyone based at Menton, since Zest also run buses serving La Turbie (Walk 6) and Roquebrune (Walk 8, alernative start). Zest also still offer printed timetables, available from the very pleasant Menton bus station just north of the gardens shown on page 86.

**Nice city buses** and the **tram** are operated by Lignes d'Azur (**www.lignesdazur.com**). Their site (English version) is very easy to use: either go to 'Plan your trip' and fill in your details or click on 'Timetables', then type in the number of the bus line recommended for the walk and download the pdf. *Be sure to look at their fare structure!* City buses/trams can be used in conjunction with all TAM intercity bus routes in the Nice Côte d'Azur municipalities, allowing you to do a lot of sightseeing for just 1.50 € (or only 1 € with a pass). Places further afield, like Menton (Walk 7) or Beuil (Walk 11), cost very little extra.

# ON ARRIVAL
## City bus/tram pass

Your first stop, still at the airport, should be the Lignes d'Azur office (the left-hand exit from Terminal 1). Buy a suitable **French Riviera pass**; there are several on offer, from 24 hours to 'multi's which give 10 trips (and can be used by more than one person) and the excellent value 7-day pass for only 15 €.

Then just take tram line 2 opposite the Lignes d'Azur office into town. Each time you board a tram (or bus), you must insert your ticket (with the arrow pointing down) into a *validating* machine (several on the tram, one behind the driver on a bus).

While you can buy your pass at the airport, they do not stock plans or timetables. For these you can call into one of the **Lignes d'Azur offices** in town — either at 4 boulevard

## The 'green corridor'

Nice's old bus station, which used to be south of the theatre, closed several years ago to make way for a 'multi-modal' transport hub near the airport (planes, trains, trams, buses, bikes and electric cars). The area from the theatre south to the Promenade des Anglais has been redeveloped into a beautiful 'green corridor', but the bus stops have been scattered all about, so **leave plenty of time to find your bus!** While the new tram lines mean much less traffic on the streets, buses and trams are now jam-packed, especially at rush hours; be prepared to stand.

Jean Jaurès or 1 rue d'Italie: see the plan inside the front cover. They are open from 08.00-19.00 Mon-Fri. Without queueing, you can pick up six plans covering all transport in the Nice Metropolitan Area and any timetables you need. But if you want to buy a pass (they offer a wide variety) or ask a question, you will have to queue. So *be sure to take a ticket when you enter:* these offices are very busy. Of course you *could* download plans and timetables from their website (see opposite), but their printed plans are much easier to read.

## Tourist information

The **tourist office** (1 on the plan), on the Promenade des Anglais near the famous Hotel Negresco (22), could be one of your first stops, to find out what's on during your visit and to pick up a **city plan**. Nearby is Balthazar (28; see page 103).

## Shopping for self-catering

Even if you are foregoing the luxury of staying in someone's beautifully equipped 'second home' in Nice (see 'Where to stay', page 8), apart-hotels should have good-quality kitchenettes with small fridges, two-ring electric burners and, more importantly, quite a good-sized oven. There is ample crockery, cutlery and cooking utensils, but you may want to pick up a few extra things, like a vegetable peeler and whisk.

Although more exotic shopping trips will come later, make your first port of call the nearest **supermarket,** to stock up on essentials. The two main supermarket chains in Nice are the Casino and the Intermarché. We blitz the nearest Casino on arrival, and stock up on staples.

But supermarkets also have delicatessens, butchers and fishmongers, and this is an easy option if you're shopping in the afternoon or on a Sunday, when the some of the local markets aren't open.

---

Supermarket shopping list reminder

washing-up liquid or dishwasher tablets
paper towels
aluminium foil
soap
tissues/toilet paper
scouring pads
salt & pepper
mineral water
milk/cream*
coffee/tea/drinking chocolate
butter*
sugar
bread*
juice
wine/beer/cider
olive oil & vinegar
eggs
tomato purée
rice
mayonnaise/mustard
torch batteries?
vegetable peeler?
whisk?

*see also panel on page 137 for gf, df supermarket products

## Markets

Once the staples are in the cupboard, the real shopping fun can begin — at the **markets**.

The huge **Marché de la Libération** on Avenue Malausséna (29 on the plan) straddles boths sides of the tram line south of Boulevard Joseph Garnier. Walk there, or take the tram to Libération. This is where the locals mostly shop (especially for

You could catch the tram here at Place Masséna and take it north to the Marché de la Libération (takes place from Tuesdays to Sunday mornings).

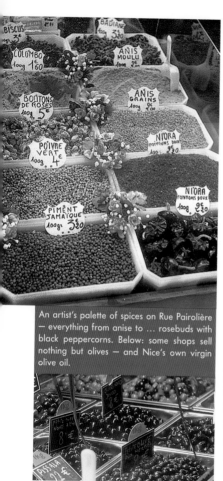

An artist's palette of spices on Rue Pairolière — everything from anise to ... rosebuds with black peppercorns. Below: some shops sell nothing but olives — and Nice's own virgin olive oil.

the freshest of fish); it's cheaper than the famous Cours Salaya market. Spend some time looking round at first, to see what's on offer, then go back to where you want to buy. If you get weary, there are plenty of places nearby for refreshment.

But undoubtedly *the* most pleasant place to shop — not only for food, but for all kinds of craftwork, is in **Old Nice**, south of Place Garibaldi (7 on the plan). Walk south out of Garibaldi on the wide Boulevard Jean Jaurès, then take the second left turn into **Rue Pairolière**. This is the main shopping street of the old town, an assault on all the senses! Whole shops are devoted to nothing but dried herbs and spices, olives, bread or soap. Not far along you pass René Socca (see page 26; 30 on the plan).

If you've come early enough and aren't ready for lunch, you might want to continue along Rue François and then fork left on Rue Benoit Bunico. Keep straight on, and you will come to the vibrant

At Christmas (and some other festivals) many 'one-man bands' set out stalls at Place Masséna. This sausage- and cheese-maker from the Pyrenees is our favourite (and we haven't even tried the 'Viagra' sausage yet!).

**Cours Saleya** (8), where there's a food and flower market every morning (except Mondays, when the whole area is given over to the famous antiques market).

Dipping your toes into a Cote d'Azur walking holiday couldn't be easier — you can start in the city of Nice, by strolling round three mini-mountains with beautiful woodlands and gardens, ancient remains and breathtaking views.

on the rooftops of nice

WALK

1

**Start the walk** at the **bus terminus** on **Mont Boron** (❶). Walk to the **area map** at the far side of the square. Two paths are just to the right of the map: take the tarred footpath to the left, the **Sentier du Cap de Nice**. This circles Mont Boron below the **old fort**, affording the fine views shown overleaf. Olive trees, holm oaks and pines shade the path-side benches. Soon views open out over Cap Ferrat (Walk 4) and its lighthouse.

When you come to a road, the path continues just to the left of it (but first cross the road, to another lovely **viewpoint** over Villefranche; ❶). Return to the path and follow it to a barrier. You are just 100m/yds short of your starting point, but it cannot be seen from here. Now take the trail that goes off left at a 90° angle, and walk round another barrier. This trail

**Distance:** 9.3km/5.8mi; 3h

**Grade:** quite easy, with few ascents; descents (mostly on steps) of about 350m/1150ft overall. Yellow PR waymarking. IGN map 3742 OT

**Equipment:** see page 9; stout shoes, sun protection, plan of Nice and information about the Colline du Château (from the tourist office).

**Transport:** 🚌 33 from 6 on the plan to Mont Boron (terminus); three hourly Mon-Sat, one or two hourly Sun; journey time about 30min

**Refreshments:** no refreshments available until you return to the port.

**Points of interest:** old forts, Colline du Château, Old Nice, views!

**Alternative walk: Sentier Littoral.** 4km/2.5mi; 1h15min. Fairly easy, but you must be agile and have a head for heights (many ups/downs, perhaps some scrambling over rocks). 🚌 38 (same frequency as bus 33 above) to the 'Villa la Côte' stop past the port — or walk there. Descend steps to Coco Beach and the coastal path (Sentier du Littoral). Follow it to Villefranche (halfway along, you have to climb steps up to the M6098 and go right until you can rejoin the path down more steps). Take 🚌 80 from the port at Villefranche or 🚌 15 from the main road back to Nice.

Nice from the Sentier du Cap de Nice

(**Circuit de Bellevue**) rounds the seaward side of the fort, circling the hill at a higher level.

When this second circuit is complete, go left on the road and follow it in a curve to the right, back to the square with the bus shelter (**35min**).

Continue along the road past the **area map**, following signs for 'Auberge de la Jeunesse'. When the road curves right, take a tarred path off left (ignore the Allée du Bois Dormant just to the left of it). Rejoin the road and continue left uphill, quickly passing the **maison forestière** on the left. At a Y-fork go right for 'Fort du

Woodland path on Mt Boron (left) and the fort on Mt Alban

Mt Alban', then cut a bend off the road by walking left through a **picnic area**. In early spring this road is a blaze of yellow-flowering tree-spurge *(Euphorbia dendroides)*. From the **Fort du Mont Alban** (**➋**; **55min**) the views down over Villefranche and its bay are superb.

Return the same way to the **area map** in the square on Mont Boron (**1h 15min**). Now descend the concreted steps on the right (**➌**; **Chemin des Crêtes**). Keep straight down through mixed woodlands, accompanied by wrens and robins, crossing straight over roads. In 10 minutes you pass to the right of the richly-decorated modern church (1927) of **Notre-Dame du Perpétuel Secours** (**➍**).

When you reach the Boulevard Carnot/M6098 *cross carefully* (blind corners). The path continues just at the left side of the Hotel Marbella, heading towards the port and the Colline du Château. Make your way to the **Club Nautique** (**❺**) and continue opposite the **commercial port** along the lovely residential Boulevard Franck Pilatte (🚌 38). Follow the road inland (signposted 'Gare'), but turn left after about 40m/yds and walk to the **pleasure port**. Circle the port on the quays, past the 'Port Lympia' terminus for tram line 1, then keep ahead to the Promenade des Anglais. You quickly come to the beautiful **memorial** to the dead of World Wars I and II on the right, its high arch carved into the **Colline du Château** (**❻**; **2h**).

Keep rounding the hill, until you come to the **lift** (*ascenseur*; **❼**), and pay the small fee to ride up to the top. (If the lift is out of action for repairs, you'll have to climb the adjacent steps; 90m/300ft.)

Colline du Château: foundations of the ruined cathedrals and artificial waterfall fed by the Vésubie River

Allow a good hour to potter about on the hill: take in the **Tour Bellanda** (●; Naval Museum), the **mosaics**, the **ruins** of two cathedrals (●; 10-12C and 14C) which once stood in the grounds of the Duke of Savoy's château, the beautiful **waterfall** (●) fed by the Vésubie ... and the views!

To return to town you *could* take the lift or adjacent steps or pick up the tourist train. We usually walk down via the cemeteries: take the steps below the waterfall, down to a road. Turn right, then take steps on the left signposted 'Cimetières, Vielle **Ville'**. From the lowest (Roman Catholic) cemetery, take the road downhill to the right, then make a sharp hairpin bend to the left on **Montée Eberlé** (➑). At the bottom, turn left for 100m/yds, to **Place Garibaldi** (**3h**; 7 on the town plan), from where you can explore Old Nice — and have some seafood at the Café de Turin (34) or a *socca* at René's (30).

## Cafe de Turin

*The* place in Nice for fish — particularly shellfish — and conveniently located at Place Garibaldi (34 on the plan), where Walk 1 ends (also near the Old Town).

Everything from the popular sea bass to 10 varieties of oyster, even sea urchins in season. An institution; always full, ensuring the freshest of food. Very popular take-away business.

---

**CAFE DE TURIN**
5 Place Garibaldi ( 04 93 62 29 52
www.cafedeturin.com
daily, all year, 08.00-23.00  €-€€€

**huge menu** with dozens of different **fish** dishes prepared to order — grilled, baked, poached, sauced

**oysters** a speciality

**seasonal seafood platters**: Atlantic lobster and crab, crayfish, snails, prawns, mussels, etc

for those who don't fancy seafood there are meat dishes and even pizza and socca

---

## René Socca

If you want to try *socca*, Nice's speciality dish, it's best to go to Old Nice, where it's widely available. We've been told that the best *socca* in the old town is to be had at **Chez Pipo** (13 Rue Bavastro, ( 04 93 55 88 82), but it's only open in the evenings (17.00-22.00 Tue-Sun, also Mon in Jul/Aug). We haven't tried it, because we prefer *socca* for lunch. (If you *do* go, get there early — waiting time for a table can be an hour or so!)

Our favourite place is **René Socca** (30); it has the advantage of being just a couple of hundred yards from useful bus and tram stops, at the top of Rue Pairolière, mentioned on page 18. There's a secret or two to eating at René's, because it is so busy!

It's a simple place — an open-fronted shop on the corner of Rue Pairolière and Rue Mirhaletti, surrounded by thick wooden tables

## restaurants

## eat

A lull at René's just before noon: the socca window is at the left (Rue Mirhaletti); other food is showcased on Rue Pairolière (at the right).

and benches. Of course in Nice it's pleasant to eat outdoors, but if it's too sunny, too cold or raining, there is also *indoor seating* — the entrance is opposite the *socca* window.

René's sells far more than *socca*, and here's our second tip. The *socca* is sold from the window on Rue Mirhaletti; all the other food is chosen from Rue Pairolière. *There are two queues, and the socca queue is by far the longer* — it stretches round the block into Rue Pairolière, so you have to try to find where it ends. Keep approaching *local* people with the word *'socca'*; if they nod, they are in the *socca* queue…

So the strategy is this: one person queues for the food,

---

**RENE SOCCA**
2, Rue Mirhaletti ( 04 93 92 05 73
**daily ex Mon from 09.00-21.00** €

**socca** (chick-pea 'pancake')

**petits farcis** (stuffed courgettes, onions, peppers)

**pizza** and **pissaladière** (pizza with onion, black olives, anchovies)

deep-fried **courgette flowers**

**aubergine** and **courgette** fritters

**cabillaud** (spicy fritters made from dried cod — Fridays only)

**fritures** (whitebait)

**sardines** and lemon

**daube** (beef stew) with polenta

**pan bagnat** (thick sandwich; the bread is moistened with olive oil and vinegar)

**tourte de blettes** (chard pie)

**sweet tartes** (apple, etc)

---

restaurants

eat

while the others find a table and order the drinks (*it is compulsory to buy something to drink if you are sitting at any table, indoors or out*).

If you are *only* having *socca*, make for the *socca* queue. But why not try some of René's other specialities (a couple of which are shown overleaf)? Admittedly, the dozens of dishes stacked up in the window look cold and rather unappealing, but as soon as you have chosen (just point to what you want), they heat it up for you.

By this time you should have moved round to the *socca* window, and the *socca* should be served in a trice, as it's coming out of the fires every few minutes. *Petits farcis* and *fritures* go especially well with *socca*. And cola or rosé wine (by the glass) is the preferred drink of the locals, although there is also Normandy cider and beer.

As you can imagine, René's also has a very popular take-away service.

# SOCCA AND *PETITS FARCIS*

### *Socca*

This recipe requires a very hot oven, which must be preheated to the highest setting available *for one hour*. Just before placing the *socca* in the oven, change setting to grill.

Put 0.5 l of water and the olive oil in a bowl, add the flour gradually, and whisk until there are no lumps (strain if necessary). Season with salt and pepper.

Spread in a thin layer (2-3 mm) on a heavily greased baking tray and place just below the grill. Heat until dark gold (5min) — or even slightly burnt. Scrape into servings and season with freshly ground black pepper.

All too much work? An easier method is to prepare the batter and fry like a pancake.

<u>Ingredients (for 4 people)</u>
250 g chick-pea (gram) flour
2 tbsp olive oil
salt, freshly-ground black pepper

recipes

# eat

*Petits farcis* (top), deep-fried courgette flowers and fritters at René's

## Stuffed vegetables (petits farcis)

Preheat the oven to 180°C, 350°F, gas mark 4. Cut the vegetables into quarters. Scoop out all the flesh and set it aside. If you are using cooked, leftover meat, poach the vegetables for about 8 minutes.

Mince the vegetable innards and mix together with the meat, eggs, garlic, parsley and cheese. Season to taste.

Fill the vegetable 'shells' with the stuffing, sprinkle the top with breadcrumbs and drizzle with olive oil. Bake for only 15-20 minutes if using pre-poached vegetables and pre-cooked meat. Otherwise bake for 30-35 minutes.

The *farcis* may be eaten either hot or cold. At René's the meat used is mostly ham, but some recipes call for minced steak, others veal or chicken. There's no reason why you shouldn't use any stuffing — or indeed vegetables — of your choice, as long as the proportions are right.

### Ingredients (for 4 people)
2 large red peppers
2 large onions
2 small aubergines
2 medium courgettes
500 g mild sausage meat or any mince or minced leftovers you fancy
2 cloves garlic, minced
2 eggs, beaten
50 g grated parmesan
fresh parsley
salt and pepper to taste
breadcrumbs (optional)
olive oil

The flanks of Mont Chauve ('Bald Mountain') are virtually treeless, so all along this invigorating ridge walk you'll have unimpeded views. The sense of isolation is wonderful, too; it's hard to believe you're at the edge of the Riviera — until you take in the panorama from the massive fort!

## mont chauve d'aspremont

# WALK

The bus trip to Aspremont, weaving up narrow roads through the hinterland hill villages, is a highlight in itself — especially as you can use your city bus pass and travel 'free'! You'll have marvellous views up to the Mercantour and across the Var Valley ... and on line 62 you'll pass through Bellet, home to one of the smallest, oldest and highly prized vineyards in France.

**Start out** at the **bus stop** (**O**) by the *hostellerie* in **Aspremont**. Walk back towards Nice on the M14 (the way the bus came in) for about 150m/yds. Past the **car park**, turn right down the **Chemin de la Vallière** (GR waymarks), taking concrete steps down into the **Magnan Valley**. Meet the M14 again in five minutes and go straight over, up a lane. In two minutes keep ahead on a stony path, then lane. At a **fork** above an isolated house (**1**; **10min**), turn sharp right uphill on the GR5. (The lane

**Distance:** 10.5km/6.5mi; 3h25min

**Grade:** moderate ascent of 345m/1130ft and descent of 530m/1740ft. Good, but stony, paths and tracks underfoot. *Almost no shade.* Red and white GR, yellow PR waymarking. *IGN map 3742 OT*

**Equipment:** see page 9; sun protection, snacks and drinks

**Transport:** 🚌 62 from Magnan to Aspremont, 08.30, 09.15, 10.35, 11.50 Mon-Fri, 08.40, 12.00 Sat. Or 🚌 76 (St-Blaise bus) from Place de la Fontaine du Temple (by Comte de Falicon 🚌), 08.50, 10.10, 11.30. Return on 🚌 35 from Aire St-Michel to Henri Sappia 🚌, every 30-40min Mon-Sat until 20.20, hourly Sun until 18.55

**Refreshments:** Aspremont (at the start), Aire St-Michel (at the end, *but this inn may be closed*); none en route

**Points of interest:**
fort on the summit of Mt Chauve
views north and south

**Alternative walk: Aspremont circuit.** 8km/5mi; 2h55min. Access and grade as above (ascent/descent of 345m/1130ft). Return on 🚌 62 at 15.50, 17.10, 18.30 Mon-Fri, 17.35 Sat. See notes on page 38.

On the way up to Fondalin in the first part of the walk, watch out for the colonies of juniper bushes. If the berries are ripe (very dark blue to black), take some home to flavour your roast lamb.

Descending from Les Templiers at the high point of the walk, you'll come upon clusters of rosemary bushes. All year round the leaves are suitable for picking.

View north from Aspremont, in spring, with the Var Valley and the Mercantour mountains in cloud.

straight ahead is the GR51, the return route for the Alternative walk.) Heading up this stony path, you enjoy a fine view back over Aspremont on its conical hill and to the perched villages of Le Broc and Carros on the far side of the Var.

Soon you pass a ruined building, **Fondalin** (❷; **35min**), in a very pleasant, grassy setting. The path rises gently through golden grasses and *garrigues* until, when you are above Nice's crematorium on the main road, the sea comes into view ahead. **Les Faces** (❸; **50min**) is the next little ruin on route. Rising below abandoned hillside terracing, you come to a final ruin

35

In spring the path is brilliantly green and gold, but the high mountains may be obscured by mist.

(**Les Templiers**; ❹; **1h**). Just 150m/yds further on, turn left uphill on a cart track, leaving the GR5. Now you are guided by yellow waymarks, with fine views down over Nice and the coast. On approaching a rock face, follow the track in a U-bend to the left and then a sharp turn to the right (where a track goes straight ahead, back towards Les Faces). The observatory on Mont Gros, as well as Mont Alban, Mont Boron and the port (Walk 1) are focal points on this stretch. The track contours above the rock face, with a fine view to the right along the Crête de Graus — the ridge you will follow back to Nice.

Meeting a road (❺; **M214, Route du Mont Chauve**; **1h15min**), follow it uphill in tight hairpins to the summit of **Mont Chauve d'Aspremont** (❻; **1h35min**). The massive old **fort** here, the last in a line of coastal defences stretching from Ste-Agnès (Walk 7) to Nice, is one of the best viewpoints in the area. The fort itself cannot be visited; it is still a working military establishment, but the coastal views are mesmerising. And

Exploring the fort and its 'moat' can be really creepy on a foggy day, but all the more fun for that!

don't forget to look back north — up towards the Mercantour and the Alps! Take time, too, to walk down around the overgrown, grassy 'moat' between the inner and outer walls.

Then retrace your steps to the GR5 (**2h15min**) and follow it left along the **Crête de Graus**. A slight rise takes you up to a **col** in about 35 minutes; ignore any minor or crossing paths; keep to the main path, heading towards a pylon. The path descends to the ruined walls of the **Château Reynard** (❼; **3h**), a shady spot from where there is another fine view. The descent now becomes more pronounced for a short time, then levels out and comes to a **T-junction** (❽). Go left, towards another pylon. At the pylon, follow the yellow PR route straight ahead; to the right are the olive groves and pines of a picnic area with tables (**Aire St-Michel**). On meeting a lane, follow it downhill past villas, to a **roundabout** on **Avenue Jules Romains** (❾; **3h 25min**). The **bus shelter** is on the far side of the roundabout, at the left of green iron gates. Don't be surprised if the bus goes into Falicon before heading south into Nice.

Below the fort on Mont Chauve

**Alternative walk: Aspremont circuit.** Follow the main walk to the **fort** (**6**; **1h35min**). Then walk back down the eight hairpin bends of the D214 (Route du Mont Chauve) and past the **track** (**5**) you took on the way to the top. After a little over 500m/yds, when you come to a **barrier** (●), take the wide waymarked path to the left. This passes a tunnel on the right almost immediately: we used to take a 'long-cut' through the tunnel, but now the eastern exit has been blocked off. So keep to the main route shown on the map. It leads via the **Baisse de Guigo** (●) back to Aspremont, with views across to the neighbouring (ruined) fort, **Tourrette**. If the waymarks are still missing at the Baisse de Guigo, look for the wide grassy downhill path just at the right of the path by which you arrived — so that you make a tight 'U'-turn to the left. Keep left at the next Y-fork. Some 500m/yds further on, the lovely grassy path deteriorates and zigzags downhill over skiddy rubble.

When you meet a cart track (●; **Chemin de la Bergerie**), turn left. This quickly becomes a lane and takes you back to the GR51 path. Follow the GR back to **Aspremont (2h40min)**.

# Hostellerie d'Aspremont

Walkers are assured a very friendly welcome in this small homely hotel. There's even a place to clean your boots!

The building was once a farm and is one of the oldest in the village. There's an open fire in the dining room in winter; in summer you'll want to eat out on the terrace — from where the views are *almost* as wonderful as from the walk itself! As you can see from the menu, local cuisine is the keynote.

Should the *hostellerie* be closed, there are a few other places to eat in the village; at least one of them should be open all day.

At the end of the walk there is a very pleasant-looking inn opposite the bus stop, the **Auberge de l'Aire St-Michel** (04 93 84 42 07; closed Wed). Unfortunately, it's only open for a set lunch (*not* in the evening) and is quite pricey.

**HOSTELLERIE D'ASPREMONT**
Place St-Claude ℂ 04 93 08 00 05
www.hostellerie-aspremont.com
closed January and Wed, Thu €-€€

**three set menus** are usually offered (all the same price); these will certainly vary from year to year, but this is a typical offering:

**menu 1**
salade niçoise
lamb stew Provençal-style (with tomatoes, onions, garlic, etc)

**menu 2**
fish soup Nice-style
chicken with crayfish sauce

**menu 3**
panned mussels, scallops and mushrooms
lamb shanks with thyme

all menus with **cheese** and **sweet**

# restaurants

# eat

## MILK-FED LAMB

Milk-fed lamb is a speciality of the hill country above Nice. This recipe is an ideal way to end the day if you've just come back from the Aspremont walk with some fresh juniper berries and rosemary! Our recipe calls for *gin*, but there is no reason why you should not use wine instead.

Around Easter milk-fed lamb (*agneau de lait*) is widely available in Nice, even in supermarkets. At other times you may have to order it in advance. But really, any nice leg of spring lamb will do.

A problem may be what size leg to buy. We usually buy just half a leg for ourselves, but to serve four people generously, buy a whole leg (and use the leftovers for stew or soup).

Legs of lamb (*agneau*) are just one of the eye-catching displays at butchers' stalls in the markets.

recipes

eat

## Roast leg of lamb with juniper, garlic and rosemary

Preheat the oven to 190°C, 375°F, gas mark 5. Rub the lamb all over, *lightly*, with olive oil. Make small incisions in the meat and insert slivers of garlic, distributing them evenly. Tuck the juniper berries and rosemary in the same 'pockets'.

Place in a roasting pan and insert a meat thermometer (if you have one). Roast for 20-25min, or until the meat starts to brown. Now pour over the gin (or wine), and continue roasting, basting once or twice, until the meat thermometer registers 140° for medium-rare. Total cooking time should be 2-1/2h but, if you prefer your lamb pink, it should be done in 2h.

Let the meat sit for 10min before carving and add the meat juices to the pan — you may want to boil them up for a few minutes to scrape up all the crunchy bits and reduce. Serve with simple roast potatoes or potato 'cake' (see page 60) and perhaps fresh peas.

Ingredients (for 6-8 people)

2.5 kg leg of lamb (*gigot d'agneau*)
4 gloves garlic, slivered
12 or more juniper berries (either dried, or fresh but ripe)
fresh rosemary
150 ml gin (or wine)
salt, freshly ground pepper
olive oil

Old trails — some dating from Roman times — are followed in this circuit via the exquisite perched villages of Peillon and Peille. Which will you prefer? Peille thrills with its *via ferrata*; Peillon is picture-postcard perfect … and home to the Auberge de la Madone!

## peillon and peille

# WALK

**Start out** at the 18th-century **fountain** in **Peillon** (**O**). Walk up the paved steps behind it, then turn left at a signpost for 'Peille Village 2h'). You pass an **iron cross** and come into olive groves, with the **Lourquière** mountain rising on the right. At a first fork, keep ahead/left for 'Peille Village' and at the next go right (same sign). There is a beautiful view back to the thimble-like spur of Peillon now, and the path enters a gorge. When a **metal gate** blocks the path (**10min**), turn s*harp left* uphill.

Eventually the old stone-laid trail passes below the red-hued climbing rocks of the **Baus Roux**, then crosses the **Galambert Stream** on a **first stone bridge** (**❶**; **30min**). Four minutes later, ignore a path forking back to the right; keep ahead. Ignore another path off right and keep ahead over a **second stone bridge** (**❷**;

**Distance:** 9.7km/6mi; 3h35min

**Grade:** moderate ascents/descents of about 500m/1640ft overall. Little shade on the outgoing path, plenty on the return. Yellow PR waymarking, but a good sense of orientation needed for the woodland paths beyond Peille. IGN map 3742 OT

**Equipment:** see page 9

**Transport:** 🚆 to Peillon. Or 🚌 to Peille (see 'Alternative routes' below).

**Refreshments:** La Voûte crêperie (📞 04 93 04 56 85) and Cauvin (Chez Nana; 📞 04 93 79 90 41) in Peille; La Madone at Peillon. See page 48.

**Points of interest:**
Peille village, its church with Romanesque belfry, and the *via ferrata*
Peillon village, the square, and the White Penitents' Chapel

**Alternative routes:** The **Circuit de Lourquière** and the path from **Peillon to La Grave** are both waymarked. You could go to Peille (Mon-Sat 🚌 116 at 10.45 from Vauban or Sun 🚌 T66 at 10.25 from Pont Michel), do the walk *in reverse* to Peillon, have lunch or tea at the Auberge, then descend to La Grave (🚌 360 at 17.35 or 🚊 Line 05 at 16.17, 18.05). Or, **on Sun only**, you could walk the entire circuit from Peille, returning on 🚌 T66 at 17.15.

The *via ferrata* where it spans Peille's gorge

**40min**; sign: 'Chapelle St-Pancrace, Peille'). Continue uphill, straight towards the masts on the Cime de la Morgelle (but this 1076m-high peak rises well to the east of your ongoing route). Tar comes underfoot in **Buampin** (❸; **50min**): keep uphill to a crossroads with a cul-de-sac sign ahead. Bend round to the right here on the Chemin de Buampin, past **iron gates** on the right. Meeting the D53 (**1h**), follow it 100m/yds to the right, then go sharp left on a path leaving from the left-hand side of a large **parking area** (❹). This takes you up to a hairpin bend of the D22. Go left and after about 180m/yds take a footpath off right.

This pretty path passes the ruined **Chapelle St-Pancrace** (❺), then descends gently through pines, back to the D53. Follow the road to the right. When the road bends right, by a rock promontory on the left (**1h25min**), your ongoing path

Peille's cluster of rose-hued buildings

dives down left just *before* the promontory. ***Note:*** *this path is badly eroded, with unprotected drops to the left; you will get to Peille almost as quickly by continuing along the D53 — a safer option.* The path (or the road) gives you some superb views of Peille's pride and joy: its well-engineered *via ferrata* — climbing walls with iron hand-holds and suspension bridge over the dramatic **Farquin Gorge**.

After crossing a stone bridge, the path rises to the **museum in Peille (1h45min)**. Once you've wandered around this beautifully-sited, sleepy village, strung out along the ravine walls, make your way along Rue Centrale (past La Voûte bar/crêperie) to Place Carnot. Take a break by the fountain or plane tree, facing the pretty restaurant Cauvin (Chez Nana) and the *mairie* (**⑥**) with its round tower. Then descend steps beside the *mairie* (**Rue du Pous**). Reaching a lane, turn right. You have joined the long-distance **Via Alpina**, but at time of writing there were no waymarks. The lane takes you to the D53, where you go left to descend its hairpins. Beyond a letterbox on the right with the number '980', you come to the **final hairpin bend** of the D53. Here your path descends concrete steps at the left (**⑦**; **2h**; still no waymarks at time of writing).

At a fork reached almost at once, take the descending path to the right (with a water pipe on your left). Keep downhill across traces of hunters' paths, passing to the left of some houses in 10 minutes and crossing the **Farquin Stream** five minutes later (❽; **2h15min**). *From here follow the notes carefully*; it is easy to get lost in these beautiful, dense oak woods. Rise up from the bridge, in five minutes ignoring a path back to the right. Ten minutes up from the bridge, ignore a large cairn on the right but, three minutes later, at an *important junction, you must turn sharp left.* (Branches are usually placed across the path straight on, indicating 'do not go this way'.) *Two minutes later, at a Y-fork, keep right* (more branches across the left-hand path). In 10 minutes the path curls round to the right at the foot of a very large **scree** (**2h40min**). Ten minutes later the path runs through pines and tall grass higher up the ridge — a very attractive setting. You pass to the left of a **ruin** (**2h55min**), then curl left towards the crests. As you push through masses of broom *(this stretch can be very overgrown in spring)*, there are some open views down right to the huge quarry at La Grave.

Rise to a **col and marker stone 128** on the right (❾; **3h05min**); keep straight ahead here, ignoring a path back to the right. Seven minutes later, at a Y-fork, keep right, quickly passing to the right of a cairn. From here the path descends gently, eventually coming to a fork: keep straight ahead (sign: 'Peillon Village'). A stone-laid trail takes you to the next fork, where you go right (same sign). At a third fork, keep straight on, retracing your steps past the **iron cross** to the **fountain** in **Peillon** (**3h35min**).

# Auberge de la Madone

This family-run hotel and restaurant is praised in all the up-market guides. Father and son do the cooking; vegetables and herbs come from their own garden. This is fine cuisine to be sampled at leisure.

They are open all day — breakfast, brunch, lunch, tea; we might start our day with a steaming mug of hot chocolate or coffee on their terrace — or end it with afternoon tea. Recently they also started doing **gourmet sandwiches** to eat at the hotel or take away.

**AUBERGE DE LA MADONE**
Place Auguste-Arnulf, Peillon ( 04 93 79 91 17
www.auberge-madone-peillon.com/en
**closed Wed and 9 Nov-31 Jan (except Christmas)** €€-€€€

**'Bistro' luncheon menu** at 19 € (starter and main course or main course and dessert) or 25 € (three courses)
**evening menus** at 40 €, 55 €, 60 €, 65 €

several different **entrées**

**main courses**, ranging from **fish** (red mullet with compote of tomatoes, purple artichokes and juice of Menton lemons) to **poultry** (guinea fowl on a polenta base, with fig and cherry sauce) to **meat** (traditional milk-fed lamb)

small but intriguing **cheese board**

eight **desserts** — like nougat ice cream with honey and grilled caramelized almonds

If you get to Peille before 2pm (or if you start there), **Cauvin (Chez Nana)** is just delightful. Open for lunch Wed-Sun (*cl* Mon/Tue) and for dinner in August); menus at 20 € and 28 €. Specialities are the buffet and raviolis. Cosy, economical **La Voûte** (*cl* Tue after 2pm and Wed) is run by a husband/wife team; freshly cooked crêpe 'pizzas', salads, bruschettas. Telephone numbers on page 43.

restaurants

eat

# CHRISTMAS-DAY PHEASANT

As amateur cooks, we're unable to duplicate any of the Madone recipes, but writing about Peillon reminds us of a wonderful dinner we enjoyed after doing Walk 3 one Christmas Day. We'd bought our pheasant the day before from the market.

Preheat the oven to 190°C, 375°F, gas mark 5.

In a heavy casserole (the one you will use for the oven), brown the pheasant pieces in the butter, then remove. Put in the onions and cook them until translucent.

Return the pheasant to the casserole and pour over *half* the brandy. Set alight and, when the flame subsides, add the stock, juniper berries, salt and pepper. Bring just to the boil, then cook in the preheated oven, covered, for about 45min.

Remove the pheasant, but keep it warm. Boil up the juices until they reduce, then add the rest of the brandy, the cream and the lemon juice. Let simmer (not boil) until you have a syrupy sauce.

If you've had time to make it, potato 'cake' (see page 60) is a treat with this dish.

Ingredients (for 4 people)
2 pheasants (ask the butcher to clean and joint for you)
1 medium onion, chopped
40 g butter
200 ml beef stock
150 ml cream
6 juniper berries
120 ml brandy (or whisky)
salt and pepper to taste
1/2 tsp lemon juice

recipes
eat

Lovely any time of year, this walk is especially enjoyable on a bright and bracing winter's day. You'll walk below the exotic gardens of some of the most exquisite properties on the Riviera, with far-reaching views out to sea and for miles east and west along the 'Azure Coast'.

## around cap ferrat

# WALK

**Begin the walk** at the **bus shelter** (○) at **St-Jean-Cap-Ferrat**. Walk back along the road the way the bus came in, heading south towards the church, with the port on your left. You rise up **Avenue Jean Mermoz** and pass the Hotel Voile d'Or on your left, then Capitaine Cook (see page 55). Take steps on the left down to **Paloma Beach**. On the far side of its restaurant you pick up a coastal walkway rounding the **Pointe de St-Hospice**, with fine views over to Eze, La Turbie, the Tête de Chien, Monaco and Cap Martin.

*After* rounding the point, take steps on the right (sign) up to the 19th-century **Chapelle St-Hospice** (❶) with its huge bronze-painted statue of Virgin and Child. An 18th-century **tower** is adjacent, but is on private land and not fully visible.

Then return to the coastal

**Distance:** 10km/6mi; 2h45min

**Grade:** easy, with ups and downs of about 130m/425ft (often on steps), *but **dangerous if wet or windy***. Little shade. No waymarks, but easily followed. IGN map 3742 OT

**Equipment:** see page 9; swimming things, sun protection

**Transport:** 🚌 15 from Promenade des Arts (6 on the plan) to Port de St-Jean (approximately every 15 minutes Mon-Sat, half-hourly to hourly on Sun); journey time 35min; returns with same frequency; or 🚌

**Refreshments:** bars, cafés and restaurants at St-Jean (start/end)

**Points of interest:**
Chapelle St-Hospice
beautifully built coastal path and adjacent properties
Ephrussi de Rothschild Foundation/Ile de France Museum (paid entrance)

**Alternative walk:** Start or end at **Beaulieu**, served every 15 minutes by 🚌 15 from Promenade des Arts (6 on the plan); 12km/7.4mi; 3h20min. Grade as main walk. A seafront walkway (**Promenade Maurice Rouvier**) runs between the marina at Beaulieu and St-Jean-Cap-Ferrat. Follow it either way to extend the walk; alight/reboard at Baie des Fourmis or Kerylos (for Villa Kerylos).

La Pinède (left) and view up to the lighthouse; below: stained-glass window at the Chapelle St-Hospice

path and turn right. Beyond the **Pointe du Colombier**, the path enters a lovely pine wood (**La Pinède**) at the edge of a little bay (**Les Fossettes**), then meets a road at a **T-junction** (❷; **1h**). Turn 90° left up-hill here (turning *diagonally* left past a 'no entry' sign for vehicles leads back to the port). Follow the road past the next little bay, **Les Fosses**.

At the next T-junction, eight minutes later, go left on a 'route privée'. You pick up the coastal walkway again and begin to round **Cap Ferrat**. Trailing superb views inland (and dodging the sea-spray), now you can really stride out, while watching the yachts and high-speed ferries sailing to and from the nearby

Menton

M33

Nice

M6098

Beaulieu-sur-Mer

Villa Kerylos M

*Baie des Fourmis*

0

N

0.5 mi

1 km

Ephrussi de Rothschild Foundation

M

M25

*Plage de Passable* **5**

**4** Lido

**6**

St-Jean-Cap-Ferrat

Mairie

M125

Pointe de St-Hospice

*Paloma Beach*

**2**

107

les Fosses

les Fossettes

St-Hospice **1**

143 ⚓ *Sémaphore*

Pointe du Colombier

100

M125

Pointe Malalongue

**3** Cap Ferrat

Pointe Causinière

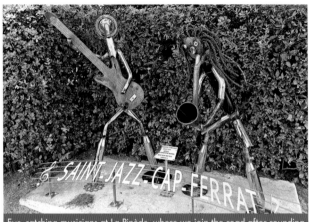

Eye-catching musicians at La Pinède, where we join the road after rounding the Pointe Ste-Hospice

ports of Villefranche and Nice. The path passes above many pretty little inlets, and below the **lighthouse** (❸; **1h40min**; paid entrance when open to the public, if you climb up to it).

After skirting the **Lido apartments** (❹) by road, the path ends at the **Plage de Passable** (**2h30min**). Climb the **steps** (❺) at the left of the beachside restaurant, cross straight over a road and go up more steps. At the next road, walk left for 160m/yds, then go right, up an alley. You emerge on the main M25 (**Avenue Denis Séméria**); the **tourist office** is on your left. Walk to the **bus shelter** opposite (120m/yds to the right) and take another alley just to the right of it. Rejoining Avenue Séméria lower down, follow it to the left, against the one-way traffic, past the **mairie** and back to the **bus shelter** (**2h45min**).

There are dozens of restaurants in St-Jean-Cap-Ferrat and nearby Beaulieu, ranging from 5-star to smaller bistros, *crêperies* and ice cream parlours. Many of the restaurants beside the port at St-Jean are open all year round and, if the day is fine, this is where everyone congregates to enjoy the lively atmosphere.

**CAPITAINE COOK**
11, Avenue Jean-Mermoz
( 04 93 76 02 66
open 12.30-14.30 and 19.30-22.30; cl all day Wed, Thu lunch, and 8 Nov to 26 Dec €€-€€€

**menus** at 30 €; à la carte 35-55 €

the **speciality** is all kinds of seafood, prepared in myriad ways

but there are **poultry** and **meat dishes**, like half chicken with mushrooms in a cream sauce, calves liver with shallots, guinea fowl (pintadeau), lamb fricassee, and various steaks

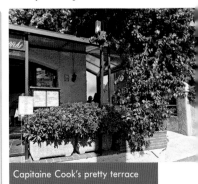
Capitaine Cook's pretty terrace

Another popular place, *not* on the harbour, is passed just near the start of the walk — **Capitaine Cook**, a long-standing seafood restaurant with a very pretty flower-bound terrace and cosy interior with some interesting paintings. It's on your left, just past the Voile d'Or. Rumour has it that it was the inspiration for the film *Casablanca* — in the 1930s it had a pianist called Sam.

There is also the informal restaurant at **Paloma Beach**, which you cross early on, but it's only open from May to September.

We sometimes go to St-Jean early in the morning and have breakfast before setting out.

## restaurants

# eat

## Taverne Masséna

Taverne Masséna (31 on the plan) is one of three restaurants in the Cresci chain, all in the heart of the pedestrian zone. Work up an appetite in advance by checking out their full menus online —it's likely they'll have whatever you fancy eating! The food is exceptionally good. On our last visit we loved the aubergine *au gratin* and the (very light) beef tartare. Their *assiette provençale,* shown left, is a good introduction to several regional specialities.

The *assiette provençale* features (clockwise from top left) *pissaladière* (Provençal 'pizza', topped with caramelised onions and black olives), a tomato stuffed with seasoned mince, *panisses* (chick pea 'cakes', not nearly as yummy as crispy socca to Pat's way of thinking), battered cod *(morue),* tomato dipping sauce, a tiny *salade niçoise* (the best and freshest Pat's ever tasted), battered and plain aubergines.

**TAVERNE MASSENA**
**25 Rue Masséna ( 04 93 87 77 57**
**www.crescere.fr; daily non-stop €€**

huge **menu**: check it out **online** at the website above

**specialities** include dishes from Alsace, with several **choucroutes**

**Sunday brunch** special at 34 € including drinks

# restaurants

# eat

# Chez Freddy

Chez Freddy (35 on the plan) is right smack in the middle of Cours Saleya, where there are dozens and dozens of restaurants. But even in the middle of a torrential downpour we're fussy: we chose it because it has a lovely view to the Palais de Justice *and* the waterfall on the Colline du Château — both illuminated at

**CHEZ FREDDY**
22 Cours Saleya ( 04 93 85 49 99
daily from 11 to 23.30 non stop €€
www.chezfreddy.com
evening menu at 25,90 €

**specialising** in fish and seafood,
6 different **aïolis** (fish stews)
6 different **paellas**
6 different **bouillabaisses**

10 **starters**, 8 **mains** (not only dishes like skate in white wine sauce, but meats like rib-eye beef),
10 **sweets**

**pastas** and **pizzas**, **sushis**(!)

**wine** by the bottle or third litre

some of their **recipes** can be downloaded from their website

night. The huge menu, with dozens of mouth-watering photos (and some recipes), can be seen and downloaded before you travel.

The spaghetti with clams was superb. Beware the *moules* as a starter: there must be over 100 mussels in this serving …

## CASSOULET DE CASTELNAUDARY

Our one-time favourite restaurant in Nice (see 'potato cake' on the next page) specialised in dishes from southwestern France. The cassoulet recipe they gave us is just too good to omit, even if we no longer recommend any restaurant serving a similar cuisine.

It's just one of many possible recipes for the most traditional and authentic of all cassoulets. One of Mère Besson's favourite winter warmers (see page 66), 'Family-style cassoulet', called for shoulder of lamb instead of duck!

It's important to use the best ingredients — this dish takes some time to cook, so make it worth while. French *confits* should be used (available back home in some supermarket chains and in specialist shops). Don't try making your own *confits* — the legs of British ducks and geese are not as fat and succulent as those reared in France. Similarly, the best dried beans are those from Tarbes (*haricots tarbais,* with their own 'appellation controlée!) or *haricots lingots* (a long, white, slightly curved haricot bean).

Soak the beans overnight in cold water. The next day, change the water let them boil for 30min, keeping an eye on the water to make sure they are always covered. Then drain the beans and preheat the oven to 150°C, 300°F, gas mark 2.

In a heavy bottomed frying pan, bring together the goose grease, oil, tomatoes, onions and garlic cloves, and cook over a low heat for 10min. Set this mixture aside. Then put the 6 *confits* into the pan and heat (again on a very low fire) until all the fat has melted. Remove the meat and set aside; leave the fat in the pan.

recipes

eat

Using the fat from the *confits*, put in the pork rind (if you have not been able to get this back home, use *lardons* sold in most supermarkets) and cook until golden brown. Remove and set aside. Still using the same fat, put in the sausage and fry gently until well browned.

Now put the tomato and onion mixture, the pork rind and the beans into an appropriately-sized casserole, together with one clove and a bouquet garni. Make sure it is all *just* covered with water. Add some pepper to taste, but *not* salt (the pork is already salty enough). Put the casserole in the oven for 1h30min. Keep watch as it cooks — the idea is to keep it topped up with enough water to *just* cover the ingredients.

After this preliminary cooking, tuck the *confits* into the beans near the bottom and the sausages into the beans near the top. Add more water if necessary, to *just* cover it all. Cook for one more hour, always keeping an eye on the water.

Serve bubbling hot, in the casserole itself. (Some recipes call for breadcrumbs to be sprinkled on top at the last minute and quickly browned under the grill.)

Ingredients (for 6 people)

1 kg dry haricots beans (preferably *tarbais* or *lingot*)

300 g tomatoes, peeled and deseeded)

1 tbsp goose grease (*graisse d'oie*)

2 tbsp groundnut oil

2 onions, chopped

6 garlic cloves

6 *confits de canard* (cooked duck, preserved in its fat)

500 g fresh Toulouse or garlic sausage

1 clove

100 g pork rind (*couennes*)

1 bouquet garni

pepper

# TWO WAYS WITH CAKES!

We became very friendly with the owner/chef of a wonderful restaurant in Nice (now sold). She made the most marvellous potato cake. This is not her recipe, but as close an approximation as we could find. The chocolate cake recipe opposite *is* her own.

## Potato cake (gâteau aux pommes de terre)

You will need a loose-bottomed cake tin 18 cm in diameter and 8-10 cm high. Preheat the oven to 220°C, 425°F, gas mark 7. Put aside four of the larger potatoes (to line the pan). Slice all the potatoes lengthwise, *as thinly as possible* (2-3 mm). Dry the slices on paper towels.

Brush the tin liberally with melted butter. Using the larger potatoes, cut a circle about 5 cm in diameter from one of the slices and set in the centre bottom of the tin. Then overlap slices all round it (see photo). Now line the edge of the tin, standing slices vertically, slightly overlapping, and making sure that about 10 mm is curled on top of the base slices (to seal the edges).

### Ingredients (for 6-8 servings)
1 kg waxy Mediterranean-style potatoes, peeled
75 g butter, melted
salt and pepper

Carefully mix the rest of the potatoes with the butter, salt and pepper. Press them tightly into the tin. Cover the lot with foil and press down firrmly against the potatoes. Bake for 1h30min (pierce

recipes

eat

with a skewer or knife to check that they are cooked). Let the cake rest for 10min before turning out *carefully*, by gently teasing the edges. Then lightly brush the top with butter and place under a pre-heated grill until golden and crisp. Good hot or cold!

## Chocolate cake (*gâteau au chocolat*)

It only makes sense to make this delicious but very large cake when you're back home, since it freezes beautifully. You will need a non-stick loose-bottomed cake tin 25 cm in diameter at the bottom and *at least* 7 cm high (the cake rises quite a lot, before falling back in when cooled). The tin should be *liberally* greased with butter and *lightly* dusted with flour or corn flour. Preheat the oven to 200°C, 400°F, gas mark 6.

Melt the chocolate with the butter. Separate the eggs and beat the whites to form peaks. Mix the yolks with the sugar until the mixture just becomes white. Using a wooden spoon, stir in the butter/chocolate mixture. Then *gently* fold in the egg whites.

Ease the cake into the pan and cook for 25min. If at this point it is still 'wobbly', give it another five minutes. Refrigerate overnight before removing from the tin. Don't mind its lopsided appearance — that is part of its rustic charm!

Ingredients (about 16 servings)

10 eggs

250 g dark chocolate (at least 70% cocoa)

250 g white granulated sugar

250 g butter

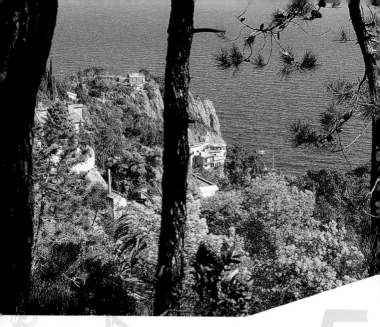

This little gem takes you into the red-rock Esterel Massif, a mass of colour all year round. Strong walkers could extend the hike: the routes marked in violet on the map are all waymarked. We end at Théoule's most popular restaurant, but you *could* return to Nice via Cannes, to have dinner at the famous restaurant, La Mère Besson.

## to the esterel

# WALK

**Begin** at Théoule's **railway station** (**O**), 1km north of the village on the D6098. While you *can* just take this road south to Théoule centre, we like to follow the **GR51**: turn right out of the station and follow the main road south for 150m/yds. Take the first right uphill, crossing the railway, then the first left downhill. Follow this lane in a little valley, round a hairpin bend to the left and back to the D6098. Turn right into **Théoule-sur-Mer** (**40min**). Then turn right off the D6098 at signs for *'mairie, poste'* (**❶**). Pass both (on your left) and keep ahead. When this street makes a hairpin turn to the left (back to

**Distance:** 11.3km/7mi; 3h40min from/to Théoule's railway station; 8km/5mi; 2h20min from the centre

**Grade:** *easy; ascent/descent of 200m/650ft overall. Some of the tracks and paths are stony underfoot; little shade. Red and white GR, yellow PR waymarking. IGN map 3544 ET*

**Equipment:** *see page 9; swimming things, sun protection*

**Transport:** 🚆 to Théoule-sur-Mer (08.23, 10.00, 11.23 daily; change at Cannes); journey time 47min-1h28min; returns at 15.11, 16.52, 17.52, 18.52. 🚌 22 runs from Théoule to Cannes at 15.10, 16.10, 17.29 (Mon-Sat *only*); journey time 30min. Or 🚗 to Théoule

**Refreshments:** *cafés and restaurants at Théoule-sur-Mer (start/end)*

**Points of interest:** *the red-rock Esterel massif (where some trails will be closed in summer due to fire risk)*

**Alternative walks:** *Prolong the circuit via the GR51/Balcons de la Côte d'Azur (violet lines on the map).*

the D6098), continue ahead on a track behind a barrier (sign: 'Col de Théoule'), rising above the railway line, into the Esterel.

*Watch carefully* for where the GR footpath heads right, off the track (**❷**; **1h10min**; you can see the railway entering the **Tunnel des Saumes** not far ahead); follow the GR, initially alongside the railway, and then above the tunnel. Rise to the **Col de**

**Théoule** (❸; **1h30min**), a major crossroads. From the col, head southeast on a *footpath* between two tracks (sign: 'Esquillon'). The path heads straight towards the Pointe de l'Esquillon, eventually widening into a road (Avenue Matisse). When you come to a junction some 40m/130ft above the D6098, turn left on a **'balcony' footpath** (❹; **2h**) and walk northeast, with fine coastal views, eventually to **Port-la-Galère**.

Tarmac comes underfoot again. Just before a junction, turn sharp left uphill on a track (❺; **Boulevard des Alpes**; sign: 'Pointe de l'Aiguille, Théoule'). Follow this until it curves west, by a wooden **barrier** (❻) on the right. Turn sharp right downhill past the barrier and, from a small open space with an area map, take the zigzag path down towards the coast. Turn left on the tarmac road at the bottom and keep

View to the Golfe de la Napoule from the Balcons de la Côte d'Azur (Alternative walk)

forking downhill to the D6098. Turn right and walk 100m/yds to the brow of the hill, then take steps on the left down to the superb rock formations at **Pointe de l'Aiguille** (**❼**; **2h45min**).

Now follow coastal paths back to **Théoule** (**❶**; **3h**). You emerge by the beachside **Marco Polo** restaurant (**bus shelter**; departures to Cannes on page 63). Or retrace your steps back to the **station** (**3h30min**).

## Marco Polo

The walk ends at the friendly, *very popular* Marco Polo restaurant (with seaside terrace and rooftop tapas bar in summer). Run by the same family over three generations. If you're too late for lunch here, take a bus into Cannes. Have an apéritif on the Croisette, then dinner at the film stars' favourite watering hole.

**MARCO POLO**
47 Avenue des Lérins ( 04 93 49 96 59
closed Mon in winter and 13 Nov-18 Dec;
open lunch & dinner €€ (1 menu at 32 €)

**fish** dishes of all kinds are the speciality (try the mixed seafood grill shown above, served with a lovely mayonnaise sauce), but there is **meat** as well, from duck to kid *(chevreau)* to steaks

morning **coffee**, afternoon **tea**, **snacks** and drinks **all day from 1/5 to 30/9**

## La Mère Besson

This restaurant opened in the 1930s and quickly became famous for authentic Provençal cooking — an 'in' place, especially during the Film Festival. 'Mother' Besson is long dead, but her devotees return year after year to enjoy dishes that made the restaurant famous. All the Mère Besson recipes in this book are authentic.

**LA MERE BESSON**
13 Rue des Frères Pradignac
( 04 93 39 59 24; closed Sun from Sep-
June, dinner only €€ (menus at 33 €, 50 €)

daily **main-course specials**; Fridays are popular for the *aïoli* — a stew of de-salted dried cod, vegetables and creamy garlic *aïoli* sauce (see recipe on page 69)

Some of the dishes which made the restaurant famous include creamy **chicken with tarragon**, *estouffade* (braised beef in red wine with onions and mushrooms), *bourride* (fish stew; recipe overleaf), **shoulder of lamb** with Provençal herbs and garlic purée.

restaurants

eat

# RECIPES FROM LA MÈRE BESSON

## Chicken with tarragon and cream
### (le poulet à l'estragon et à la crème)

Mère Besson's recipe (available on the current menu at the restaurant) calls for deboned chicken, but this is not necessary. If the chicken *is* deboned, reassemble the legs and wings with a wooden skewer or string. Put some of the tarragon leaves in boiling water for a few seconds, then rinse in cold water, drain and pat dry; add these at the last minute, thus retaining the colour.

In a frying pan just big enough to hold all the pieces, bring the oil to a high heat, then turn down a bit. Fry the chicken, turning, until just golden (about 6-7 minutes).

If there is any excess oil in the pan, pour it out. Add the wine, salt and pepper and tarragon. Let this cook gently for 20 minutes, partly covered, to reduce.

Now add the mushrooms and cream and let it reduce again — the sauce should be fairly thick. Best served with white rice.

Ingredients: (for 4 people)
1-1.2 kg chicken, cut up (and preferably deboned)
olive oil
3 sprigs fresh tarragon
150 ml dry white wine
100 ml crème fraîche
150 g button mushrooms, minced
salt and pepper to taste

recipes

eat

## Provençal fish stew *(bourride)*

This dish is a white *bouillabaisse*. If you start from scratch, it's a bit of a production! We've included both the full version and a 'cheat's version' of both the *court bouillon* and the *aïoli*. La Mère Besson's recipe did *not* call for potatoes or carrots, but we like it this way, and our cookery editor would add leeks and celery too!

Put the *court bouillon* and vegetables in a large heavy-bottomed pan. Cover, bring gently to the boil and cook gently for about 10min. When the vegetables are almost done, add the fish; cook for another 8-10min.

Put the fish and vegetables in a tureen or casserole and keep hot. Strain the *court bouillon* and, if necessary, add more water, until you have 600 ml of liquid. Whisk the egg yolks with a tiny bit of cold water into which you have dissolved the cornflour, then whisk in 150 ml of the *aïoli*. Pour on a little of the *court bouillon* and whisk together well.

Return to the heat and cook gently, stirring all the time, until the sauce thickens. *Do not let the sauce boil, or it will separate.* (If this should happen, you'll have to blend the sauce at high speed, strain it and reheat in a clean pan.)

### Ingredients: (for 4-6 people)

1 kg firm white fish, cut into large pieces
400 g waxy potatoes, cut into thick slices
150 g carrots, cut into thick chunks
300 ml *aïoli*
2 egg yolks
1 level tbsp cornflour
fresh parsley to garnish
toast or croutons to serve

Pour the sauce over the fish and vegetables. Put the bread or croutons in the bottom of (pre-warmed) soup bowls, and add some of the fish mixture. Pour over some of the sauce and garnish with fresh parsely. Serve the rest of the *aïoli* separately.

recipes

eat

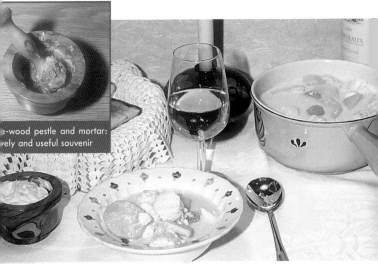

-wood pestle and mortar:
vely and useful souvenir

## For the *court bouillon*

Simmer together for 45min:
600 ml water, 150 ml white wine,
1 sliced onion, 1 sliced carrot, 1 sprig
each of fennel, parsley and thyme,
1 bay leaf, 2 tbsp minced celery,
1 slice of lemon, 2 garlic cloves,
1 tsp salt and 6 black peppercorns.
Then strain through a fine sieve.

**OR** just buy some fish stock, like
Joubère, available in several UK
supermarkets!

## For the *aïoli* (garlic mayonnaise)

Set aside 300 ml olive oil. Crush
together 4 garlic cloves and 1/4 tsp
salt. Beat in 2 egg yolks. Add some
oil, a few drops at a time, beating
constantly. When this thickens, add
1 tbsp lemon juice. Slowly add the
rest of the oil, beating, and 2 more
tbsp lemon juice. Add pepper to taste.

**OR** simply crush the garlic with the
salt, then stir into a really good,
bought mayonnaise!

On this walk you will have some of the finest views on the whole of the Riviera. You rise gently along the north side of the Grande Corniche crest, with a superb outlook to the Mercantour mountains. After crossing the shoulder, you enjoy a magnificent coastal panorama for the whole of the plunging descent.

la turbie and èze

WALK

The walk begins at the *mairie* (**O**) on the main D2564 road, the **Grande Corniche**, in **La Turbie**. Cross over the road to the Hotel Napoléon, then turn left. After 450m/yds, at the roundabout, ignore the D2204 off right to the motorway; cross staight over towards 'Nice' and walk past a cylindrical **pillar with an iron cross** on the top (on your right). Some 250m/yds from the roundabout, turn right up the **Chemin de la Forna** (**10min**; walkers' signpost). There are fine views back to the Trophée des Alpes as you climb.

As the tarmac runs out, keep straight ahead on a cart track (sign: 'Cime de la Forna'), to pass to the right of a **reservoir** (**20min**). Just before a **second, square reservoir**, turn left up another stony cart track (sign). In two minutes keep straight ahead

**Distance:** 8km/5mi; 3h15min

**Grade:** easy ascent of 155m/510ft, but strenuous descent of 600m/1970ft. Little shade. Yellow PR waymarking. IGN map 3742 OT

**Equipment:** see page 9; walking pole(s).

**Transport:** 🚌 116 to La Turbie from Vauban (Mon-Sat at 10.45), 🚌 T66 Sun from Pont Michel at 08.55, 10.25, 12.45, 14.00); journey time 40min; daily returns from Eze-Bord-de-Mer by 🚌 100 (every 15min) or 🚆 (half-hourly at 9 and 39 min past the hour)

**Refreshments en route:** cafés and restaurants at La Turbie (start) and Eze Village (halfway)

**Points of interest:**
La Turbie and the Trophée des Alpes (see page 74; closed Mondays)
Eze Village
Riviera views straight out of a film!

**Shorter walk: La Turbie — Eze.** 6km/3.7mi; 2h20min. Fairly easy, but steep descent of 280m/920ft. Walk as far as Eze Village, return by 🚌 112 at 15.25, 17.30 or 19.40. Avoids final 320m/1050ft of steep descent.

**Alternative: La Turbie circuit.** 8.5km/5mi; 2h50min. Easy ascent; access by 🚗 or 🚌 as above (returns at 15.35, 18.05 Mon-Sat, 15.20, 17.15, 18.55 Sun). See page 73 at 1h40min.

(**❶**; **sign:** 'Fort de la Revère'). *(The Alternative walk returns via the 'Cime de la Forna' path to the left here.)*

Now a lovely path through tall grass takes you along the northern flanks of the **Grande Corniche**, just below the crest.

You look north to Utelle, where a chapel teeters on the edge of the cliff, and the mountains of the Mercantour. The Fort de la Revère crowns the rise to the west, above two forestry park buildings. From here the frenetic jockeying for position at the motorway toll booths (*Péage*) below seems a world away.

On meeting the U-bend of a track, turn left uphill (❷; **sign:** 'Fort de la Revère'). You emerge at a large doline (basin) and the **Maison de la Nature** (❸; **1h25min**), with an interesting little museum, well-landscaped gardens, and picnic tables. Before continuing towards Eze, walk downhill to the coastal overlook (with benches) and follow the **corniche track** for short way. After five minutes, just before the **first tunnel** (❹), a *sentier botanique* (with a *table d'orientation*) turns sharply up to the left — a possible detour. Continue through the **second tunnel** (❺; **1h40min**), to take in the superb coastal panorama.

(*For the Alternative walk*, continue along this track, eventually forking left to a water tank on the **Cime de la Forna** (●). Fork left again, to descend a stony path back to the reservoirs, and from there retrace your steps to La Turbie. See violet line on the map.)

La Trophée des Alpes: built in 6BC from almost pure-white local stone, it originally rose to 50m/165ft. It stood on the Via Julia Augusta, in commemoration of Roman victories over 44 different Alpine tribes. Sacked at the end of the Roman Empire, the trophy was mined by the troops of Louis XIV and then used as a quarry (La Turbie's church incorporates some of its stone); a museum relates its skilful restoration in the early 1900s.

To continue the main walk, retrace your steps to the Maison de la Nature and start walking up the road towards the **Fort de la Revère**. But after less than 100m/yds, turn left down a path (sign: 'Eze Village'). This pretty path descends through tall grass above some luxurious villas (after 350m/yds ignore a path down to the left). On coming to a concrete drive, follow it downhill to the right. Keep right, downhill, at further junctions, until you meet the **Grande Corniche** again (**2h 05min**). Cross *carefully*, turn right for 20m/yds, then turn left down a lane (**Chemin Serre du Forque**). The shade of pines is welcome here,

Begin here at the arcaded *mairie* in La Turbie, crossing to the Hotel Napoléon (the Café de la Fontaine is just to the right).

but the descent is *very* steep. Keep straight down — by tar, path or steps, until you meet the **Moyenne Corniche** (M6007), opposite the entrance to **Eze Village** (**6**; **2h20min**), where there are cafés and a **bus shelter** 50m/yds to the right. End the Shorter walk here, or take a break before, knees a-tremble, you begin the final descent.

Cross the road and head up into Eze, passing the **tourist office** on your right. Just past the **Fragonard** shop on your left, you will turn left down the **Chemin Frédéric Nietzche** (**7**; **sign:** 'Eze Mer'). But first join the crowds and walk on through this enchanting village — to visit the tropical gardens, church and White Pentitents' Chapel (just below the Nid d'Aigle restaurant).

Nietzche's wide old mule trail (he climbed it every morning from his house on the coast) descends in gentle zigzags through a surprisingly wild valley (**Vallon du Duc**) above deeply-cut *calanques*. Eventually the path turns right, crosses a **col** (**2h50min**) and makes the final descent — with fine views over Cap Ferrat. When you meet the M6098 (**Corniche Inférieure**) at **Eze-Bord-de-Mer**, turn right to the **bus shelter** (**8**). Steps to the **railway station** (**9**; **3h15min**) on the south side of the road are just 60m/yds further on, behind an eastbound bus shelter.

## Le Café de la Fontaine

Should you be doing the Alternative walk and missing out Eze, *do* visit Le Café de la Fontaine. By the fountain a short way to the *right* of the Hotel Napoléon (where the walk turns left), it's usually open from 7am — a great way to set yourself up for the walk! You could have a superb gourmet lunch or dinner here for just 30 €, but in fact we ate more inexpensively, choosing just one dish and some wine. The menu changes daily, depending on what is in the market. And the place is very casual — you won't feel

**LE CAFE DE LA FONTAINE**
4 Av du Général de Gaulle,
La Turbie ( 04 93 28 52 79
www.hostelleriejerome.com; click
on 'le cafe-de-la-fontaine'
open daily for lunch and dinner €€

**starters:** vegetable soup with *pistou*, cod *brandade* with sweet peppers or fresh raviolis with peas

**entrees:** rabbit à la niçoise or roast leg of lamb

**desserts:** bitter chocolate tart, prune pudding with armagnac or peach tart with verbena

out of place in walking gear, despite the fact that it's owned by the very swish Hostellerie Jérôme (with two Michelin stars). Outdoor tables with wind breaks — even warm in winter!

## Le Nid d'Aigle

Being such a tourist magnet, there are restaurants galore in Eze. Unless you just want an ice-cream, give the ones near the main road a miss and walk up to the very top of the village. Here you'll find the welcoming Nid d'Aigle, a homely place with stone and wood décor, Provençal fabrics on the tables, and fantastic views over the village rooftops to the sea. In fine weather you can eat out on the terrace, under the shade of a venerable mulberry tree.

The Sauvage family have run the restaurant for decades under

## restaurants

# eat

The cosy interior at the Nid d'Aigle, just before lunch time. Everyone is still out on the walled terrace, enjoying the fine autumn weather.

the guidance of Mme Marie; her daughter Dominique is married to the head chef, Fabrice. The short (winter) menu shown here doesn't really do justice to the delicious food: the lamb fillets are served in their own juices, subtly flavoured with rosemary. The fish may have a sauce of tomatoes, coriander, basil, lemon, saffron and olive oil. On their website is a slideshow of 25 of their dishes.

**LE NID D'AIGLE**
1 Rue du Château, Eze ( 04 93 41 19 08
**www.leniddaigle-eze.com**
**open daily from 09.00-21.30** €€

wide range of **drinks, sweets, snacks all day**

**breakfasts** served till 11.30

nine **entrees** — salads, *escargots*, charcuterie, *soupe au pistou*

three kinds of **fish**, depending on the season

**meat**: lamb, pork, steak, beef tartare rabbit (see photograph on page 79)

**tagliatellis** with different sauces

# NEW YEAR'S DAY RABBIT

We worked up such an appetite when rabbit was on the menu in La Turbie at the start of the walk that we made this dish at our apart-hotel the following New Year's Day. We ordered a fresh rabbit in advance from the market —this is highly recommended, but you *can* buy packaged whole rabbits or rabbit pieces (legs or saddle) in all French supermarkets.

## Caramelized rabbit with lemon *(lapin au caramel et citron)*

Preheat the oven to 190°C, 375°F, gas mark 5. Coat the rabbit pieces with the sugar. Melt the butter in a large frying pan, add the rabbit and cook gently until the sugar has caramelized. Then set the meat aside.

Add the lemon juice and a little stock to the pan and use a wooden spoon to deglaze (scrape any flavourful bits clinging to the pan into the liquid). Then set aside this mixture aside separately.

*If you have a cast-iron casserole, the rest of the preparation can be done in it, but if you only have a pyrex casserole (as is usual in apart-hotels), continue by cleaning out the frying pan and using it again.*

Heat the oil, add the *lardons,* and cook gently until fairly crispy, then set aside, leaving the oil and bacon fat in the pan. Put in the onion, carrots, and garlic and fry gently until softened. Add the liquefied cornflour, remaining stock, tomato purée, wine, lemon juice with deglazed pan bits, and the grated lemon rind. Using a wooden spoon, stir constantly until this comes to a boil. Then turn down and simmer until it reduces to a shiny glaze. Add salt and pepper, and the *herbes de provence,* stir, and turn off the heat.

recipes

eat

One winter Sunday when we set out, rabbit was the day's special at the restaurant in the Hotel Napoléon opposite the *mairie*. It inspired us to create this recipe, which we often make at home. But since then, we've enjoyed superb rabbit at Le Nid d'Aigle. This photograph is of their rabbit dish, *not* ours.

Put the rabbit, lardons and liquid mixture into a casserole and stir to mix. The liquid should just cover the meat (if it does not, add more wine!).

Cover the casserole and place in the preheated oven for 50min to 1h. When it is cooked, the meat should be falling off the bone.

With a slotted spoon remove the rabbit pieces and other large bits and set aside on a preheated serving dish.

Simmer the remaining liquid if necessary, until it reduces. Add the port and cream and reheat (but don't let it boil!). Adjust the seasoning and pour the sauce over the rabbit.

## Ingredients (for 4 people)

1.5 kg rabbit, jointed
75 g caster sugar
50 g butter
4 tbsp lemon juice
300 ml vegetable stock
1 large onion, finely chopped
2 tbsp olive oil
100 g diced rindless streaky bacon, unsmoked (lardons nature)
1 garlic clove, crushed
1 tbsp cornflour, liquefied in 1 tbsp cold lemon juice
2 tsp tomato purée
grated rind of one lemon
2 carrots, sliced
150 ml red wine
1 tsp *herbes de provence*
3 tbsp port
3 tbsp cream
salt and freshly ground pepper

The tangle of old cobbled lanes at Ste-Agnès, woven below arched passageways, evokes medieval times. But while this 'highest of Europe's coastal villages' has always been important strategically (the fort was the most southerly defence of the Maginot Line), no road was built until 1933. This walk follows an old mule trail.

## st-agnès and castellar

# WALK

**The walk begins** at the **Col St-Sébastien** (**O**), 200m/yds below **Ste-Agnès** by footpath, at the junction with the D22 to the Col de Gorbio. There's a **medieval chapel** here, a **fountain**, and a barrage of signposts. Follow the old cobbled footpath descending below the chapel, the GR51 (sign: 'La Virette, Monti, Castellar'.) Sometimes horses are kept in this area; if you encounter any electrified fences, use the insulated handles to open and close the gates.

As you descend into the wilderness of the **Borrigo Valley**, it's hard to believe that you're just a short way inland from the busy coast. At the outset you pass a stand of cypresses that once gave welcome shade to travellers

**Distance:** 8km/5mi; 2h45min

**Grade:** easy-moderate ups and downs — about 500m/1640ft of descent overall and 270m/885ft of ascent (of which 200m is at the end of the walk). Red and white GR waymarking. *IGN map 3742 OT*

**Equipment:** see page 9; stout shoes, sun protection

**Transport:** 🚌 100 from Port Lympia (near 11 on the plan) to Menton's bus station (every 15min); journey time 50min. Change to 🚌 10 to Ste-Agnès (08.05, 09.50, 12.25, 14.25 Mon-Sat, 09.05, 12.55 Sun/holidays); journey time 40min. Return to Menton on 🚌 6 from Castellar to Menton's bus station (15.40 daily, also 17.55 Mon-Sat or 17.35 Sun/holidays); journey time 30min.

**Refreshments en route:** restaurants and/or cafés at Ste-Agnès (start) and Castellar (end)

**Points of interest:**
villages of Ste-Agnès and Castellar, their craft shops and artists' studios old mule trails

ascending to Ste-Agnès (and now hide a sewage farm), then descend to the grassy banks of the **Borrigo** (**1**), a lovely place to while away an hour or three ... *(Be sure to turn sharp right here; do not follow what may look like a more obvious path straight on.)*

When you come to the **stream crossing** (❷), you may find horses slaking their thirst and encounter another electrified fence. Look ahead now to your destination — the honey-hued buildings of Castellar, strung along a ridge.

The old stone-paved mule trail up to Castellar

You pass through a rock chaos in a grove of trees (obviously a popular, shady picnic spot) and then another rock chaos. Beyond a small stream bed, you rise to the ruined hamlet of **La Virette** (❸; **35min**).

Descending steeply from the ruins, watch carefully for the GR 'change of direction' sign and turn *sharp left* downhill, *ignoring* any yellow waymarks. Cross another stream (in the **Ravin de Merthea**) and rise quite steeply, past a short narrow section with a drop to the right. As you head southeast on the far side of this ravine, look back to Ste-Agnès, where its strategic position on the rocky escarpment is evident. Your eye will also be drawn to the motorway below, and the Monastère de l'Annonciade at Menton.

Dip into yet another little gully, the **Ravin de Cabrolles** — a cool glen in summer, where ivy twines round the trees. Having climbed up the far side, a wide cobbled trail comes in from the left behind you; here you look straight down on Cap Martin (Walk 8). Keeping to the GR, ignore any offshoots left to houses. You more or less contour above a huge fenced-off cemetery, until the track swings north in a U-turn. Ten-15 minutes later (750 metres futher on) a **fork to the right** (④) takes you back onto a path.

On coming to a concrete-surfaced T-junction, turn right. Steps take you down to the **church** at **Monti** (**5**; **1h45min**). Cross over to the **Auberge Pierrot Pierrette** (once one of our favourite places to eat, now sadly out of business), then turn sharp left just past the **bus shelter**; your concrete path continues just behind it (although it looks as if you are walking straight into someone's property!). Descend towards an industrial area but, just before reaching it, go straight ahead along a **track** (**6**; just past a huge pylon). Walk to the left of a glass and breeze-block wall (a swimming pool; it belonged to Pierrot Pierrette).

Now you start to round the final large valley before Castellar, the **Torrent Careï**. Immediately after crossing the **Careï** (**7**), keep left uphill at a Y-fork. Then, just as you start to rise on concrete steps, fork right on a path, through a pretty, wooded section. Cross another stream and, on meeting a concrete road, follow it uphill to the left. But a short way up, fork sharp right on a concrete path (**8**; **sign**: 'Castellar').

Cross another stream and, at a fork, keep left uphill (sign: 'Castellar 1h'). But fork right just 15 paces along. The path climbs in easy zigzags, sometimes through vineyards, and with an excellent view to Castellar on the approach. On coming to a crossing concrete lane, turn left uphill to a **chapel** on the Avenue de St-Antoine in **Castellar** (**2h45min**). Follow the road uphill to the right, then take steps up right, into the heart of the village. At the top of the steps there is an **iron cross**; opposite is the **bus shelter** (**9**) .

*Photograph opposite:* Like St-Agnès, Castellar is home to many artists and artisans. In this Italianate village, the *trompe l'oeil* influence is pervasive.

Because we always stopped in Monti for a terrific lunch, we never visited any restaurants in Ste-Agnès or Castellar.

And both of our choices in Menton have closed as well! So we tried **La Coupole** € (☎ 04 93 35 76 73), a very homely restaurant, well sited almost opposite the casino, on the Avenue de Verdun (the road to the bus station). It's been going for 35 years, family run. The menu is wide-ranging, and it's open for lunch and dinner 7/7 all year. The *sangría* was lovely on a hot day, but Pat was disappointed with her wilted *salade niçoise* and overcooked veg. We had better luck at Le Big Boss (page 91).

restaurants

eat

Menton at Christmas, on the Avenue de Verdun, just south of the bus station. The
north towards Castellar and Sospel, further north, are clear as a bell. Some tree
painted with 'snow', others hanging heavy with oranges. But Menton is chiefly know
lemons, with a lemon festival in February. Menton's lemon pie is a must!

# A LEMON FESTIVAL TARTE

## Menton lemon pie *(tarte aux citrons de Menton)*

Prepare shortcrust pastry and leave in the fridge for 30min-1h. Preheat the oven to 190°C, 375°F, gas mark 5, with a baking tray on the middle shelf. Roll out the pastry and carefully place in an 22 cm pie tin, then bake for 25 minutes, until it is golden and crispy.

While the pastry is baking, prepare the filling. Gently warm the milk. Mix together the egg yolks, sugar and flour.

Using a wooden spoon, gradually stir the milk into the egg mixture. Then add the lemon juice and grated peel. Thicken this mixture in a double boiler (bain-marie) or a bowl placed over a saucepan of boiling water.

Cool the filling. Whisk the egg whites with a little sugar until peaks form and the mixture begins to glisten. Spread the filling over the pre-cooked pastry and cover with the egg whites. Return to the oven and bake until the egg whites become golden (about 10min).

Ingredients (for 8 servings)

shortcrust pastry, made in
    advance, or ready-made
4 large eggs, separated
80 g caster sugar
2 tbsp plain flour
500 ml milk
juice and grated peel of
    3 lemons

recipes

eat

Cap Martin is to Menton what Cap Ferrat is to Nice — an exclusive enclave of the seriously wealthy. But their coastal paths are accessible to everyone, so for a while you can be 'master of all you survey' — the princely views are free.

## cap martin

# WALK

**Start the walk** at the **railway station** (**O**) for **Roquebrune-Cap-Martin**. Cross the tracks via the underpass, then turn left and make your way over to the coastal path, '**Le Corbusier**' (**5min**). Rounding the first inlet, the 'path' is a narrow, airy metal walkway (with handrails) clamped to the vertical side of the cliff. Trailing fine views back to

**Distance:** 7.8km/4.8mi; 1h45min

**Grade:** easy, with gentle ups and downs, mostly on a concrete walkway. IGN map 3742 OT

**Equipment:** see page 9; bathing things (for Carnolès), sun protection

**Transport:** 🚆 to Roquebrune-Cap-Martin (half-hourly; see sncf. com) or 🚌 100 (every 15min from Port Lympia) to the '2ème Escalier', a bus stop on the D6007. Descend steep steps beside the bus stop to a lane, turn right, then turn left down 'Sentier conduisant à la gare'. (Allow extra time for this steep descent/ascent). Return the same way. Or 🚌

**Refreshments:** restaurants on the coast from Cap Martin to Menton

**Points of interest:**
coastal path and views

**Note:** You could begin by visiting the hill village of **Roquebrune**, with its ancient castle, have lunch, and then descend steps 250m/820ft to the coast, to begin the walk (🚌 21 from Menton at 08.50, 11.10, 13.15, 15.15 Mon-Sat; 09.00, 11.00, 13.30 Sun; alight at the stop called 'Lavoir'.

The coastal walkway

Monaco, you pass several spurs down to the sea, but swimming is not allowed: the sea is at least 10m deep and the rocks very sharp. (The path is named in memory of the architect, who *drowned* while swimming off these rocks.)

You pass below the **Villa Cyrnos** (❶), once the home of the Emperess Eugénie, where Winston Churchill came to paint and dine. Finally you round the tip of the cape, with fine views over to Menton. The path then ends at the **Boulevard Winston Churchill** (❷; **55min**). Retrace your steps from here. With views focussing on Monaco, Cap Ferrat, the Tête de Chien, La Turbie and the inland hill village of Roquebrune, return to the **Roquebrune-Cap-Martin railway station (1h45min)**. Or walk on into Menton, past the splendid Plages de Carnolès, where you *can* swim, perhaps before enjoying lunch at Le Big Boss.

Since we usually walk here in winter, when the coast east of Cap Martin tends to be quiet (except for the February festivals), we either go back to Nice or on to Menton for our evening meal. But if you start the walk at **Roquebrune**, you may want to have lunch there. For a light meal, try La Grotte, carved into the rock and with tables in the beautiful square — everything from snacks to hearty fare (3 Place des Deux Frères, ( 04 93 35 00 04, closed Wed and last week of Oct; €).

## Le Big Boss

This place, right on the seafront, 450 metres west of the casino, is ideal if you walk into Menton after rounding Cap Martin … perhaps after a swim? We were not expecting anything special in 'just another tourist haunt' and were very surprised by the high quality of the perfectly cooked cheeseburger and the ham salad with the freshest of greenery and tomatoes. The service was super-friendly, too.

Menton's port

LE BIG BOSS
seafront promenade ( 04 93 28 17 60
Fri-Wed non-step till late €-€€

**snacks, paninis, burgers, crêpes, waffles** — but some **pastas** as well

a **speciality** is a very large selection of herbed home-made **sausages**

delightful and copious **salads** with the freshest of vegetables or fruit

**ice-creams** are another speciality

restaurants

eat

# TWO WAYS WITH FISH FILLETS

Inspired by a delicious meal at a now-closed restaurant in Nice, we found some turbot recipes … but no turbot. These recipes work well with halibut, John Dory, sole or dorade, more easily found in the UK.

## Turbot (or halibut, etc) in sparkling wine
### (turbot au champagne)

Preheat the oven to 190°C, 375°F, gas mark 5. Unless you have an electric blender, take the time to chop the onions and cress very finely. Melt the butter in a pan and fry the onion gently until soft. Add the chopped watercress and fry for a further 2 minutes, stirring constantly. Stir in the warm milk; add salt and pepper to taste. Bring to the boil, then lower the heat, cover, and simmer for 15 minutes. Then rest at room temperature.

While the sauce is simmering, lay the fillets (flat, not overlapping) in a large, well-buttered baking tray. (If all you have in rented

### Ingredients (for 4 people)

4 large fish fillets, ideally turbot or halibut
50 g butter
1 medium onion, finely chopped
1 bunch watercress (keep a bit to garnish, remove stalks and chop the rest)
300 ml warm milk
salt and freshly ground black pepper
1 bay leaf, torn in 4 pieces
300 ml sparkling white wine

recipes

eat

accommodation is a roasting pan, first line it with foil.) Season the fish to taste and place a bit of bay leaf on each. Pour over the wine, then cover with buttered foil and bake according to the thickness of the fish (allow 8min for each 10 mm thickness). Remove the fish with a slotted spatula, discard the bay leaves, and set aside on a warm platter. Cover with foil; keep hot.

Ideally one now purées the wine from the fish with the milk/cress/onion sauce in a blender, but this is not mandatory. Instead, add the warm wine to the sauce a little at a time and, stirring constantly, reduce over a high heat. Adjust the seasoning and pour over the fish. Garnish with the watercress sprigs.

## Turbot (or halibut, etc) à la provençale

Quantities and cooking times/temperatures for this recipe (from La Mère Besson) are much the same as opposite. Make (or buy) a *court bouillon* (see page 69) using a bouquet garni, some minced shallots, lemon juice, salt, pepper and white wine. Set aside and chill.

Place the fish in the liquid in an oven dish (remember, if you overlap the fish, the cooking time will be longer). Bake according to thickness, or until it flakes easily. Then remove and keep warm.

Strain the cooking liquid and reduce over a high heat in a heavy pan. At the same time sauté quickly a handful of minced button mushrooms and add these to the reduced sauce. Whisk together one egg yolk with a tablespoon of cream, and whisk it into the sauce to thicken. Pour around the fish. Garnish with the tomatoes (*tightly clustered*) and parsley.

Ingredients (for 4 people)
4 large fish fillets (ideally turbot, halibut, John Dory)
*court bouillon* (see page 69 and ingredients above)
1 egg yolk
1 tbsp cream
100 g button mushrooms, minced
salt and pepper to taste
2 tomatoes, skinned, deseeded and diced into 1 cm cubes
some fresh parsley, chopped

No trip to the south of France is complete without a journey on the delightful Train des Pignes (perhaps named for the pine cones the locals collected on Sundays to take back home; theories vary). Not only is the journey a splendid way to see the mountains, but a very pleasant way to get to Walks 9 and 10.

## train des pignes

# EXCURSION

After the County of Nice was returned to France in 1860, there was great interest in linking the newly re-won Alps with the coast. Every valley wanted its own train. One of the surprisingly numerous projects to get off the drawing board, despite obstacles of terrain and financing, was the line built from Nice to Digne between 1890 and 1912 — spanning 150km with 16 viaducts, 17 bridges, and 25 tunnels, one of them 3km long! Some other railways built at this time, at enormous cost and effort, have not survived: the viaducts on the line to Barcelonnette are now drowned beneath the Lac de Serre-Ponçon; the Caramel Viaduct (which can be seen as you rise up the old mule trail to Castellar during Walk 7) is the sad remains of the route from Menton to Sospel.

This is a 'friendly' train; it

**Departures:** from Nice daily at 06.55 and 09.25; back from Digne at 14.25, 17.35. Journey time 3h25min. There are other departures north and south from Annot: see www.train provence.com/english for timeables and prices: click on 'Nice > Digne', then 'Times and Fares'. The same operators, Chemins de Fer de Provence, run a touristic steam train between Puget-Théniers and Annot. Note: departures are from 3 on the plan, *not* from the main SNCF station.

**Hints:** The little train is very comfortable, with 'sightseeing-size' windows. Travelling south, sit on the left; travelling north, sit on the right. *Don't* make the mistake of sitting in the front row — the ticket collector monopolises the front windows! Take a map, to pinpoint all the sights en route. The train stops for a good five minutes at Annot, where those 'in the know' take a break at the pleasant station restaurant. *Be warned:* If you are based in Nice, you won't even have time for a long lunch in Digne unless you take the first train of the day. But it's a very relaxing way of sightseeing — so we just pack a picnic. If you enjoy walking from the train, you can download a brochure (in French) of 5 other walks from the train at their website (click on 'excursions' > 'walking tours').

ALPES-DE-
HAUTE-PROVENCE

Allos,
Colmars

St-Martin-
d'Entraunes

Via

Sisteron

Thorame-
Haute

Verdon

Guillau

Digne-
les-Bains

Font-Gaillarde

Méailles

N85

Bléone

Châteauredon

Thorame-
Haute-Gare

10 Grès
d'Annot

les Mées

N85

St-André-
les-Alpes

Annot

Train des Pignes

Barrême

Entreva

Moriez

N202

Col de
Toutes Aures

Lac de
Castillon

Demandolx

Moustiers-
Ste-Marie

Castellane

St Auban

Valensole

Point
Sublime

D4085

le
Logis

Tho

Riez

la
Palud

Route Napoléon

Seranon

D6

Aix

Lac de
Ste-Croix

Corniche Sublime

Verdon

**Grand Canyon
du Verdon**

Comps

Mons

Baudinard

Plan de
Canjuers

Montmeyan

Bargemon

Aups

**Fayence**

VAR

Callas

Cal

Tavernes

Tourtour

Barjols

Salernes

Bagnols

Toulon

**Draguignan**

Parc National du Mercantour

Valberg  Beuil  **11**  St-Sauveur-sur-Tinée  le Boréon  Madone de Fenestre  **Tende**

St-Martin-Vésubie  Vallon de la Gordolasque

Gorges du Cians  Tinée  Belvédère  **12**

Puget-Théniers  **9**  D6202  Toüet  la Bollène  Col de Turini

Madone d'Utelle  Utelle

Train des Pignes  Var  Vésubie  **ITALIA**

Bonson  Plan-du-Var  Sospel  **7**  Castellar

Aiglun  Sigale  Roqueston  ALPES-MARITIMES  Ventimiglia

Esteron  Aspremont  **3**  Peillon  **8**  Menton

Coursegoules  Carros  **2**  A8/E80  la Turbie  Cap Martin

Vence  **6**  Roquebrune  Monte Carlo

Gourdon  le Bar  D6007  Èze  **1**  D6098  Beaulieu  **4**  Cap Ferrat

St-Vallier  Cagnes  **Nice**

Grasse  D6185

Cézaire  D6185

Lac de St-Cassien  Antibes

Juan-les-Pins  D6098

8/E80  **Cannes**  Cap d'Antibes

sterel  **5**  la Napoule  Théoule

**N**

97

*Entrevaux — a magical village you can visit with the Train des Pignes*

will stop to drop off or pick up walkers virtually anywhere along the run. If you download their brochure of five walks (or better still, find one of their old *books* with *many* walks from the train — perhaps in a market, perhaps online), do remember that the trails vary enormously in interest and difficulty and *should not be attempted without the relevant large-scale IGN map!*

Leaving Nice, the train moves like a tram through the city and into the suburbs. Soon it's hurtling along the wide basin of the **Var River**. At **Colomars** look up left, above the industrial spread of modern-day Carros beside the river, to Carros-Village and Le Broc perched on the hillside. At **St-Martin-du-Var**, the **Esteron Valley** comes in from the left. Beyond **Plan-du-Var**, don't miss the mouth of the **Vésubie Gorge**, seen through the Pont Durandy on the right. The perched village of **Bonson** rises on the left. Now you're in the **Defilé du Chaudan**, between the two carriageways of the D6202, racing the motorists. Just beyond a tunnel look out right for the towering walls of the **Tinée Gorge**, backed by the mountains of the Mercantour. Colourful smallholdings introduce **Toüet-sur-Var**, huddled below a rock cliff. Then the most magnificent of all the gorges opens up — the **Cians Gorge** (Excursion 2 takes you up this gorge). Alight at **Puget-Théniers** for Walk 9, or continue past a 5km-long stretch of orchards and plane trees lining the way to **Entrevaux**, the fairy-tale village shown opposite.

Past the gap of the **Daluis Gorge**, watch for some high bluffs on the right: Walk 10 rounds a ledge almost at the very top (see photograph on page 112). At **Annot** notice the houses built into boulders like those shown on page 110 (the '**Grès d'Annot**') and

The little train (a 'romantic' older carriage shown here at Annot station) runs all year round. In winter it's equipped with a snow plough. The only time it stops is when there is one of the (fairly frequent) strikes!

the chaos of *grès* just as you leave, as well as the *robines* (see page 107). Now the train hurtles through the rolling fields and orchards of the ver- dant **Vaïre Valley** to **Méailles**.

A 3km-long tunnel precedes **Thorame- Haute-Gare**. Still the little train tears along, shrugging off the fact that it has already climbed 1000m from Nice! The gorgeous **Verdon Valley** is followed to **St-André**. You have a fine view of the church and the **Lac de Castillon** as you leave — watch for paragliders here.

Following the **Asse de Moriez**, come to **Moriez**: just outside it there are interesting rock dykes. A 12th-century chapel rises on a hill outside **Barrême**, where a huge fir graces the station. Now the N85 (**Route Napoléon**) is just beside you on the right, and you skirt the **Forêt Domaniale des Trois Asses**, as you follow the Asse de Blieux via the **Clue de Chabrières** (on the left) to **Châteauredon**. From here the train curves north and crosses the wide **Bléone River**, before coming into **Digne**, below the Alpes de Haute-Provence. Out of the station, turn left to walk into the town (about 15 minutes).

We can't tell you anything about restaurants in Digne; we haven't gone that far for years. We either leave the train to walk from Annot (restaurants below) or Puget-Théniers (see page 108 for one of our all-time favourites).

Or we just take the train to marvel at **Entrevaux**, where there's a hotel-restaurant just by the station: Le Vauban (℃ 04 93 02 13 05; closed Sun evenings and all day Mon from Nov-Easter; menus from 22 €). The décor is warm and homely; the menu includes seasonal dishes of *daube,* wild boar, or even sweetbreads — as well as *secca* (dried salt beef with olive oil and lemon juice, a local speciality). The terrace (shown right) has fine views towards the Entrevaux setting. If you visit on a day when they are closed, ask at the tourist office (℃ 04 93 05 46 73) about other restaurants when you pick up some leaflets about this magnificent site.

If you go on to **Annot** for Walk 10, there are several hotels with restaurants, at least one of which will be open out of season. Ask at the tourist office. We show *approximate* closing dates. Out of the station, take the road into the village. You pass L'Avenue, on the left (℃ 04 92 83 22 07, closed 16/12-13/2). Not much further along, turning right on the main road you come to the main square where the hotel Beausejour (℃ 04 92 83 21 08) has a pretty restaurant indoors and an outside terrace for summer months. The tourist office is on the left here. On the far side of the square, behind the war memorial, is the Café du Commerce (℃ 04 92 83 21 49, all year, lunch and dinner). We've never been here, but since our favourite restaurant has closed, we looked for another. This looks very tasty indeed, judging from photos on the web, so we're keen to try it.

## restaurants

# eat

# DAUBE A LA PROVENÇALE

In case you missed *daube* at Le Vauban in Entrevaux, try this easy recipe. *Note:* not all recipes call for wine vinegar, so only add this if

you want the extra, slightly sour 'kick. Cut the meat into 3-4 cm cubes and marinate overnight with one onion, one carrot, the cloves, thyme and bay, salt, pepper, wine (and vinegar).

Preheat the oven to 180°C, 350°F, gas mark 4. Remove the meat from the marinade. Brown it bit by bit on all sides in a heavy-bottomed pan, transferring each lot of meat to a heavy casserole. Then fry the *lardons* and, when they are browned, add the garlic, carrots and onions. Swish all this around, then add to the casserole.

Add the stock, tomato purée, salt and pepper to the casserole. Cover and cook for 1h, then reduce the heat to 140°C, 300°F, gas mark 2 and cook for a further 4-5h, until the meat is meltingly tender. Pour the liquid into a separate pan, boil down to reduce to a shiny sauce, then pour back over the *daube*.

### Ingredients (for 6 people)

1.5 kg lean beef, like shoulder
(*paleron de boeuf*) or, even
better, shin (*jarret de boeuf*)
100 g bacon bits (*lardons*)
3 medium onions, sliced
4 medium carrots, sliced
3 garlic cloves, crushed
50 ml wine vinegar (optional!)
4 level tbsp tomato purée
6 cloves
sprig fresh thyme, 2 bay leaves
salt and pepper to taste
500 ml red wine
200 ml beef or vegetable stock
olive oil or lard for browning

recipes

eat

# Balthazar

We first found this place when we were staying up in the wilds of Puget-Théniers (see Walk 9) in cold, rainy weather. We took the Train des Pignes to Nice and just headed for the sea! The nearest bright lights shone at a café on the corner of Halévy and the Promenade, just a few doors east of the tourist office. Called Balthazar (28 on the plan), its setting looking out to sea is perfect, and plenty of seating outside lets you make the most of it. Although it's not a 'restaurant' proper, there's plenty of choice for a full meal.

Balthazar is not inexpensive, but the food is very tasty.

**BALTHAZAR**
3 Promenade des Anglais ( 07 61 02 09 04
daily from 08.00-19.00 €€

**English breakfast** — or continental — from 08.00 till noon

a **speciality** is **tapas** — chicken wings or fingers, jalapenos, mozarella or cheddar sticks, onion rings, mixed tapas

**club sandwiches** and **burgers**

**salads** — niçoise, caesar, smoked salmon, tomato and mozzarella, goats' cheese

enticing **meat and cheese platters**

savoury and sweet **crêpes, ice creams**

**fish & chips**, **escargots**, **moules farcis**

huge selection of **drinks**, **cocktails**

Pat's favourite — *moules farcis with chips*

restaurants

eat

103

This walk is a good introduction to the *robines* of Haute-Provence. Ranging in colour from off-white to black, they have an austere beauty. It also affords superb long-range views along the orchard valley of the Var, to say nothing of the opportunity to pick up local goodies at the superb tourist office by the station.

above puget-théniers

WALK

**Start out** from the **railway station** at **Puget-Théniers** (**O**). Turn right on the main road, then left to the village centre. Take steps at the right of the **post office** up to **Rue de la Redoule** and follow it to the **cemetery** (**❶; 15min**). From walkers' signpost 174 follow a path uphill, cross the road to the cemetery, and continue to the left of the telephone exchange (with the word 'judo' on the wall!). Keep left at a fork, after 200m/yds joining a fire-fighting road, which quickly becomes a track. Before the track makes a U-bend, be sure to *turn back sharp left* uphill on the way-marked route — a **centuries-old trail** (**❷**). Climbing in

**Distance:** 4.5km/2.8mi; 2h

**Grade:** moderate climb/descent of 330m/1100ft, but you must be sure-footed and have a head for heights. Avoid the walk in mist, strong winds and wet weather. Some of the paths cross *robines* (see next page), where *care is needed.* Yellow PR way-marking. *IGN map 3641 OT*

**Equipment:** see page 9; walking pole(s), sun protection

**Transport:** 🚂 to Puget-Théniers (Train des Pignes; departs Nice 06.55, 09.25, 13.05 daily from 3 on the plan); journey time 1h20min. Returns at 16.27, 19.38. Or 🚗 park at Puget-Théniers railway station.

**Refreshments:** cafés and restaurants at Puget-Théniers; none en route

**Points of interest:**
Puget-Théniers (Maillol statue, Romanesque church, castle site)
*robines* (see caption on page 107)
steam train to Annot on Sundays in summer (enquire at the station)

zigzags, you enjoy fine views over Puget-Théniers and can trace the Var Valley from Utelle in the east to the castle at Entrevaux in the west. Reaching a **crest**, walk (*carefully*) along the very top of the *robines* pouring down into the **Ravin du Planet** on your right.

Before long, the path moves away from the edge and heads

The knife-sharp Castagnet Cliffs above Puget-Théniers

west, leaving a little ruined house up above to the right. From a **pass** (**1h**) you look ahead into the Roudoule Valley, backed by the Crête d'Aurafort. As the walk continues uphill in tight zigzags, be sure to locate your waymarks. The **Roche d'Abeille** (**1h15min**) marks the top of the climb: from here there is a magnificent view east along the Var. The 'Bee's Rock' is a natural fortress, from where *robines* pour down into the Ravin du Planet. Walk on to signpost 173 and, at the fork, keep straight ahead, to the ruined **Bergerie de Lava** (❸; **1h20min**), where you can take a break on the grassy slopes.

The onward walk starts from the back of the *bergerie* and descends to the **Roudoule Valley**, with views to the Crête d'Aurafort, the Castagnet Cliffs and the roofs of Puget-Théniers. This narrow path is especially beautiful in autumn, when wine-red Venetian sumac and gold grass contrast with the dark shiny leaves of the holm oaks. Here again, *care is needed* on the *robines*. Finally the path crosses a very **narrow ridge** (❹) between two *robines* — this only lasts for 50m/yds, but is potentially dangerous on a windy day — and amazingly, this is when you return to 'civilisation' and are just above a house!

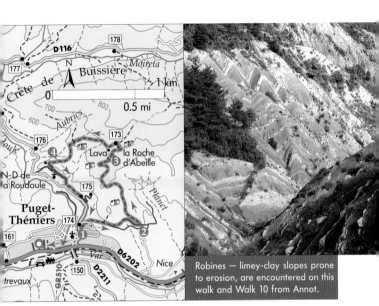

Robines — limey-clay slopes prone to erosion, are encountered on this walk and Walk 10 from Annot.

Join the drive to the house and, where it curves to the right, turn sharp left on a lane. When this lane turns towards a house after 150m/yds, continue down a rough, grassy trail, making for the cemetery and telephone exchange. As you approach a wooden gate, turn sharp right down a footpath. Cross a gully on a **wooden footbridge** and come to the **Rue de la Roudoule** (and signpost 175; **1h50min**). Turn left, follow the road down to sign 174, and head back to **Puget-Théniers station (2h)**. Before leaving, take time to visit the splendid tourist office next door. Not only are there leaflets, maps and books, but it is also a 'Maison du Pays' — a 'supermarket' of local produce!

## L'Oustalet

This restaurant, next to the station at Puget-Théniers, might go unnoticed if you make straight for the centre (it's housed in the old station *buffet*). *Don't* miss it! It's a *very* popular, excellent restaurant specialising in local dishes. We drive up from Nice or come by train just for lunch. They are open almost all year. It's very cosy in winter, but in fine weather we like to watch the comings and goings of the Train de Pignes or the steam train, so we sit beside the railway line, out on the terrace shown in the photo.

We're quite thrilled to read all the excellent reviews about L'Oustalet on Trip Advisor and other sites because we think we were the first to 'discover' this place when Marilyn and Yann opened it and publicise it to an English-speaking audience. Just look at the photos on their new website!

**L'OUSTALET**
by the station ( 04 93 05 04 11
www.oustalet222.wixsite.com
cl Sun after 3pm €-€€ (menus at 14 € for 2 courses or 16.50 € for 3
open 09.00-14.30, 16.30-19.00

huge, sophisticated selection, from

**light meals**: sandwiches, omelettes, *secca* (the Entrevaux speciality mentioned on page 101), and 8 kinds of *bruschetta*

**fresh pastas**; 10 different sauces

**fish** including locally-caught trout, sea bass, sole

**meat** from duck to veal, sweetbreads, goulash of wild boar, *daube*, steaks with varied sauces

## restaurants

eat

The Puget-Théniers tourist office/ 'Maison du Pays' is a treasure-trove of home-made local delicacies. You can buy whole prepared meals here in glass Kilner jars, and rest assured that there are *no additives or preservatives*. Here's one of the dishes we bought that was fairly easy to duplicate at home.

## Mutton (or lamb) stew with chestnuts *(Navarin de mouton aux châtaignes)*

Brown the bacon bits in the olive oil, then add the garlic and cook for one minute. Set aside. In the same pan, brown the meat on all sides. Return all the meat to the pan, add the brandy and flame it, to burn off the alcohol. Then add the wine and bring just to the boil.

Transfer the meat/wine to a casserole, stir in the stock, beans, chestnuts, tomato puree, herbs, bay leaf, and salt and pepper to taste. Cook in a slow oven (160°C, 325°F, gas mark 4) for 2h30min. (If you prefer your beans and chestnuts more 'al dente', stir them in for just the last hour of cooking.)

Like all stews, this tastes better when reheated (at 200°C, 400°F, gas mark 6) for 35 minutes.

Ingredients (for 4 people)
800 g boneless mutton
  or lamb, cubed
100 g unsmoked bacon
  bits *(lardons natur)*
400 g haricot beans
100 g prepared chestnuts
200 ml red wine
200 ml stock
2 garlic cloves, crushed
1 tbsp tomato paste
1 tbsp olive oil
2 tbsp brandy
1 tsp *herbes de Provence*
1 bay leaf, in pieces
salt and pepper

recipes

eat

This magnificent walk, beautifully shaded by oaks and chestnuts, takes you through a chaos of towering eroded sandstone boulders and rock arches, the Grès d'Annot. Midway through the hike you skirt a cliff-face below massive rock 'totem-poles', high above the confluence of the Vaïre and Coulomp at Les Scaffarels.

grès d'annot

10

WALK

**Start out** at the **railway station** at **Annot** (◉): head downhill towards the village, then turn right and walk through a **tunnel** under the railway (sign: 'Circuit des Grès d'Annot, Chambre du Roi'). Turn right again on a stony track, passing the octagonal water tower for the old steam trains. Keep along to the last railway building (past a house above left, built into the first of the *grès* en route), where the tracks disappear into a shed (sign: 'Annot, Escalade sur les Grès'). Just past the sign, meet a fork and go left, climbing slightly.

When you are directly above the turntable for the old

**Distance:** 5km/3mi; 2h15min

**Grade:** moderate climb/descent of 330m/1100ft, but you must be sure-footed on the *robines* (see photograph on page 107). Avoid the walk in mist or wet weather. Yellow PR waymarking. IGN map 3541 OT

**Equipment:** see page 9; walking pole(s), sun protection

**Transport:** 🚂 to Annot (Train des Pignes; departs Nice 06.55, 09.25, 13.05 daily from 3 on the plan); journey time 2h. Returns at 16.00, 19.10. Or 🚗 park at Annot station.

**Refreshments:** cafés, restaurants and hotels at Annot (see page 101)

**Points of interest:**
attractive old town of Annot
the Grès d'Annot
*robines* (see photo on page 107)
steam train to Puget-Théniers on
  Sundays in summer (enquire at the
  station)

steam locomotives, be sure to turn left in the first zigzag of this **stone-laid mule trail** (❶; **10min**). Climb into the rock chaos, where climbers have inscribed mythological names on the sandstone boulders. Paths thread out in all directions; *keep careful watch for the yellow waymarks.* If in doubt, whenever possible follow paths running parallel with the Vaïre Valley on the right (climbing southeast); don't head too far left. Beyond

Rock 'totem poles' above the confluence of the Vaïre and Couloump

the chaos you should find yourself on the stone-laid trail again (**30min**), soon crossing some *robines* (clay slopes) shored up with logs. Five minutes later more *robines* are crossed and there is a fine view to terracing on the far side of the Vaïre.

At a crossing of paths (**50min**), climb up to the right (sign: '**Chambre du Roi**'). In the shade of beautiful chestnuts you reach the **narrow defile** shown on page 110 (❷). As you start into it, look right: 'entree' is written on a stone. If you're slim enough, and not claustrophobic, squat down and crawl through this opening, into the three huge rock 'rooms', illuminated by a small gap high above. Then return and continue through the towering, shady defile. At the end of the passage you come to a **clearing** with a fireplace and boulder-benches — a lovely rest spot.

The path continues up to the cliff-edge above the confluence of roads and streams at Les Scaffarels, from where a fabulous **'balcony' path** (amply wide, but watch your footing and *take special care* on windy days) carries you east in the setting shown opposite (**3**; **1h05min**), with beautiful views of innumerable cliffs and the Galange Gorge. Once round the bluff, there are more breathtaking views over the apron of emerald cultivation skirting the Var. You now head inland through once-cultivated chestnut groves, which are losing ground to the faster-growing pines. (Soon a signposted path on the right indicates a possible detour north-northeast to a magnificent **viewpoint** (●) over the Coulomp Valley. It's 15 minutes up and 10 minutes back down; *not* included in our times; *take care; the drops are sheer!*)

The main path climbs gently over bedrock and then through a mossy glen, full of ferns and tall trees embraced by ivy. You pass to the right of a ruined **stone shelter (1h20min)** built below an overhang of rock, with a venerable chestnut in front. Now the path climbs quickly to the **Pas des Portettes**, the highest point of the walk. Turn left downhill here, passing under a high **rock arch (❹)**. Descending, follow the path round a bend to the right. As you come into another rock chaos, enjoy the lovely play of light and shade, as the sun streams through the magnificent chestnuts onto the moss-covered boulders. Once in a while, the path climbs *very slightly* before descending again, but *be sure not to climb too far up to the right.*

Some seven-eight minutes below the pass, watch for your **turn-off (❺)**: you must go *sharp left* downhill. (If you find yourself walking north above Annot, you've gone too far.) Further downhill, several springs gush out over the path. which can be very wet at times, but it's pleasant to walk accompanied by the sound of running water.

You pass a building on the left dated 1672 and two minutes later come to the 12th-century chapel of **Notre-Dame-de-Vers-la-Ville** on the left (❻; **1h55min**). Its wall-belfry is surmounted by a stone cross. From here a grassy stone-laid trail takes you downhill in zigzags, past the **14 Stations of the Cross**, each embellished with a naïve painting on glazed tiles. Cross the **railway line** and follow a lane between colourful gardens and fields. When you come into **Annot**, take a break for some refreshments, then head back on the main road, following 'gare' to return to the **station (2h15min)**. Perhaps when you get back to Nice you'll have time to try the easy recipe opposite.

# OSSO BUCCO NICE-STYLE

The Italian influence is everywhere evident in the cookery of Nice, no more so than this popular dish which gets its 'twist' from the addition of lemon (and, if you like, orange) zest. This is another recipe from La Mère Besson (see page 66).

Our recipe is a bit of a 'cheat's' osso bucco; we've used tinned (Italian plum) tomatoes. Heat the olive oil in a large, heavy-bottomed frying pan *with a lid*. Dust the meat with flour and brown lightly on both sides.

Turn down the heat. Add the onion, garlic, tomatoes and salt and pepper to taste. Pour over the wine and sprinkle with the zest.

Let all this cook slowly, covered, for 30min, then remove the lid and leave to simmer for another hour or more. While you are enjoying an apéritif or two, reminiscing about the Annot 'totem poles', the flour and marrow from the meat will merge with the wine to create a good sauce which should have reduced to perfection.

Serve with white rice or boiled potatoes.

### Ingredients (for 4 people)

4 thick veal shins (*jarret de veau*) with marrow
1 small onion, finely chopped
2 garlic cloves, crushed
400 g tin chopped tomatoes
200 ml dry white wine
grated rind of 2 lemons (and half an orange)
flour to dust
4 tbsp olive oil
salt and freshly ground pepper

recipes

eat

This excursion — like the Train des Pignes — makes a wonderful day out, with a visit to the most spectacularly colourful gorge in the south of France. Beuil is a lovely walking base for most of the year, although the skiers take over in winter.

## gorges du cians

EXCURSION

Ideally you will be sitting on the right-hand side of the bus as it pulls out of the *gare routière*, but make sure the windows are tinted, as you will be on the sunny side. The initial part of the trip follows the same route up the Var Valley as the Train des Pignes, so keep an eye out for all the sights mentioned on page 99.

After about an hour and a quarter, beyond Touët-sur-Var, the bus leaves the N202 and heads up the D28 through the honey-coloured

**Departures:** 🚌 770 from Nice Gare/ Poste (just at the left of 2 on the plan) to/from Beuil; out at 09.00, returns at 16.40 daily; journey time 1h50min. Alight at the tourist office. *From Jul-Sep there is also a daily walkers' 'Randobus' from Vauban (32 on the plan) daily at 07.30; returns at 17.10: book it at www.lignesdazur.com.*

**Points of interest:** The bus follows the same route as the Train des Pignes as far as the Cians Gorge: see notes on page 94. The highlight of this trip is the beautiful Cians Gorge.

**Refreshments:** cafés and hotel-restaurants at Beuil (see page 125)

**Hints:** Travelling north, sit on the right-hand side of the bus; travelling south, sit on the left.

chasms of the lower **Gorges du Cians** and below the small village of Rigaud. If you think this lower gorge is spectacular, wait till you see what lies ahead!

The first landmark of any note as you climb up this lonely stretch is pretty **Pra-d'Astier**, gateway to the upper gorge. Just after leaving the hamlet there is an abrupt transformation in the landscape: from honey, the rock colour changes to red — rust red, blood red, wine red. The contrast between the rock and the varying greens of the moss, ferns and trees is breathtaking.

Below is the rushing turquoise-to-emerald **Cians River**.

The river drops some 1600m/5250ft on its 22km descent from Beuil to the Var, and has left the towering red schist chasms in its wake.

Watch for signs alerting you to the **Petite and Grande Clues** — the most spectacular rifts. The D28 has been diverted through tunnels in both places, allowing sections of the curving old road to be converted into pedestrian walkways with spectacular views (see opposite).

When you get to **Beuil** you should have plenty of time to enjoy Walk 11 and take some refreshment in one of the cafés or hotels (see page 125).

While we try to avoid the eyesore development of most ski resorts, Beuil is an exception. Its setting is just stunning. There are several waymarked walks around this alpine village, but we're convinced that this circuit shows it off to best advantage, whatever the season.

above beuil

WALK

**Start out** at the **tourist office** (*syndicat d'initiative;* ○) on the main D28 road in **Beuil**. Walk down the road (signposted to the Gorges du Cians). Some 300m/yds downhill, at walkers' signpost 52, fork right for 'Circuit de Bramafan'. Then fork left 50m/yds along. The cinder track soon rises in zigzags, to a **shrine** on the right (❶; signpost 53; **15min**). Continue straight ahead at this junction, ignoring the cart track to the right (your return route). Rising gently on the northeastern flanks of the **Plateau St-Jean**,

**Distance:** 8.4km/5.2mi; 2h45min

**Grade:** easy-moderate, with ascents/descents of 320m/1050ft overall. Little shade. Yellow PR way-marking; some short cross-country sections (no path) are marked with wooden sighting posts. *IGN map 3640 OT*

**Equipment:** see page 9; sun protection

**Transport:** 🚌 770 to Beuil (for details see page 117 and alight at the tourist office); or 🚗 park at the tourist office on the main road (D28).

**Refreshments:** cafés and hotel-restaurants at Beuil (see page 125); none en route

**Points of interest:** alpine surroundings Beuil village

you have fine views back to Beuil and down left into the **Cians Valley**, with the little St-Giné chapel on the far bank.

At a Y-fork by some buildings (just past the shrine), keep left, on the main track. Beyond the hamlet of **Le Serre** (❷; **25min**), you cross a stream. Beuil disappears from view, but Les Cluots (2106m/6907ft) in the southeast now attracts your attention: its summit is almost always snow-capped. **Rétouria** (❸; **45min**) is another pretty little hamlet, with wooden-roofed stone houses and a good view down south towards the Cians Gorge.

At **signpost 56** (❹) you come upon another handful of

houses. Go *left* here, for 'Cians', leaving the 'Bramafan' circuit and zigzagging down towards the road in the Cians Gorge. When you reach **signpost 56a** (**5**; **55min**) 60m/200ft downhill, turn right at the Y-fork (signposted towards 'Bergians Soubran'). This narrow and slightly overgrown (but well waymarked) path gently regains the height lost, as it rises to another group of houses and a wooden signpost: 'Itinéraire Pédestre'. Here you come to a Y-fork at a **barn** in the middle of the hamlet (**6**; **1h10min**). Take the fork to the left of the barn and walk down the overgrown path to the stream bed. Rise up the far side for about a minute, then take a faint path to the right. After 10m/yds the path is clear, with yellow flashes on the trees. Soon the path contours above fields, before coming into a patch of forest and then climbing gently through a stream bed wilderness.

Rétouria and (right) the little shrine encountered some 15 minutes along

At the **Fuont Nouvelle** (**7**; **1h25min**) a cart track comes in from the right. Continue to the left of this well on a stony path, still rising up the stream bed. At a fork three minutes along, go right, now climbing a bit more steeply. You pass to the left of a **concrete plinth** (take either path at the fork here). Then walk to the left of a wooden **sighting post**, making for the top of the ridge ahead, where the next sighting post is visible (no way-marks).

Having risen to a crossing track, follow it to the right, to **signpost 57a** (**8**; **1h42min**). From here head northeast towards 'Bergians Soubran', crossing a grassy **plateau**, with a 'top of the world' feeling. Giant thistles and thousands of sheep accompany you, as well as views north to the jagged peaks of the high Mercantour. The hamlet of La Fuont is below to the right.

Nearing **Bergians Soubran** you'll surely encounter goats, sheep, geese, hens, cows, horses, cats and dogs! At the **Collet du**

All the little hamlets are beautifully kept; in autumn the wayside is decorated with blooms — seemingly just for the pleasure of walkers!

Guérin (❽; **1h55min**), where there is a **cross** on the left and signpost 57 on the right, take the cart track to the right of the lane. The landscape is a blanket of golden grass interwoven with strands of firs and spruce.

Cross the lane about 350m/yds further on and go straight ahead down a wide grassy path at the left edge of the woods. It drops straight down to a grassy track and signpost 54 (**2h10min**). Go half-right here, once again following the 'Circuit de Bramafan' and passing between two cottages at **Pra Premier** (❾). At a Y-fork, keep left downhill, straight towards Beuil. Soon the trail peters out, but just keep steeply downhill through the grassy field, towards a **metal pole** with a yellow flash. There is a beautiful view over the green valley of **La Condamine** and to Beuil.

More sighting posts lead you onto a cart track descending from the right. Follow this downhill to the left, to a huge **cairn**. Continue downhill at the left of the cairn on an old trail flanked by the remains of stone walls. Reaching the **shrine** first passed at the 15min-point (❶; **2h25min**), turn left, back to **Beuil** (**2h45min**).

There are a several restaurants in Beuil. Closing dates are erratic; they open for the summer walking season and again for the winter skiing season, closing in spring and autumn. Our favourite place to eat, the very friendly Hotel l'Escapade, is open all year round, but otherwise *avoid November,* when you may go hungry!

**HOTEL L'ESCAPADE**
**Beuil centre, on the main road to**
**the church ( 04 93 02 31 27**
www.hrlescapade.fr
**open daily all year round**
   **restaurant open 12.00-14.00**
      **and 19.30-21.00**
   **€-€€ (menu at 26.00 €)**

   **entrees** include the beautifully presented **assiette terroir**, which you serve yourself from platters brought to the table — *terrine de foie de volaille* (chicken liver and mushroom), sliced brawn (head-cheese) and cured ham, various pickles, and huge jars of wild *sanguin* mushrooms in olive oil

**fish** course features **local trout** in basil sauce

**meats** include steaks, *daube de boeuf* (thickened with corn starch), tripe sausage *(andouillette)*

wide range of **pastas** and **petits farcis** (see page 31) for a lighter meal

The Escapade (mentioned in Michelin) features regional cooking. You can see their dishes on their website (under the search icon, key in 'menu'). We usually eat here à la carte, because we can't manage more than the 'entrée' — the *assiette terroir* — a meal in itself. The dining room is very cosy in winter, but there's a pretty terrace for fine warm days.

## restaurants
# eat

# CHESTNUTS AND CHARD

If you spend any time in the Mercantour National Park (Beuil is on the doorstep) no doubt you'll come across some menus using either chestnuts *(châtaignes)* or Swiss chard *(blettes)*. Here are a few popular recipes (all for four people). We've cheated by using prepared chestnuts — of course fresh would be better, if you have time!

### Chestnut purée *(purée de châtaignes)*
Using packaged prepared chestnuts, simmer them very slowly with some salt and fennel leaves for 30 minutes. Then purée, adding milk (to the consistency of a bread sauce). Lovely with veg, poultry or a roast.

### Chicory with chestnut purée *(endives sur purée de châtaignes)*
Prepare the purée as above and keep warm. Halve 4 heads of chicory lengthwise and braise in stock and a little butter for 20min. Grease a baking dish, add the purée and smooth out. Place the cooked leaves on top, dotted with butter. Grill for a few minutes, until the top is brown.

### Chicken with chestnuts *(poulet aux châtaignes)*
Roast a chicken with sage and salt in a *covered* roasting pan. While it is cooking take some prepared chestnuts and simmer them in salted water with fennel leaves, celery, sage, a clove, and caraway seeds for 30 minutes, then strain. When the chicken is cooked, remove it and keep it warm. Put the chestnuts in the pan and roll them around gently in the chicken juices. Carve the chicken and serve with the juices and chestnuts from the pan.

You'll see chard pie *(tourte de blettes)* for sale in Old Nice, for instance at René Socca. Surprisingly, this is a *sweet*, flavoured with lemon, sugar, dried raisins and pine nuts. Just look at the size of the chard on sale in France! This slice of the pie, from René's, was about the same size as this book!

Here's a 'ratatouille'-type recipe for this versatile vegetable. But what do you do with the leaves? You make a *tourte de blettes* — or a chard omelette (another popular dish), served with fresh shaved parmesan.

*Tourte de blettes*

### Chard stems Provence-style (côtes de blettes à la provençale)

Sweat the onions in the olive oil. Add the tomatoes and let it all simmer for 15min over a very low heat. Then add salt, pepper and the thyme. Put in the anchovies and let them break up and melt.

Boil the chard stems for 10min. Add them to the onions and tomatoes. Let this simmer for 5min, then add the garlic and chopped parsley.

### Ingredients (for 4 people)

1 kg Swiss chard; this recipe uses the stems only, chopped (out of season, pac choy would be a good alternative)

1 onion, minced

500 g fresh tomatoes, deseeded and cut into small pieces

2 anchovy fillets

2 garlic cloves

1 tbsp olive oil

sprig each of parsley and thyme, chopped

salt and pepper

recipes

eat

127

Turini! One of the first places we make for when we arrive at Nice. Surrounded by magnificent forests of firs and spruce, this eyrie is as silent and refreshing as a Christmas morning snowfall ... except when there's a motor rally on the famous hairpin road!

cime de l'arpiha

WALK

**Start out** at the **Col de Turini**: walk north on the D68 (the road to the Authion, signposted 'Camp d'Argent'). After 700m/yds, at signpost 234 (**15min**), turn left. Follow this motorable track to the **Vacherie de Mantégas** and signpost 235. From July to September you can sample and buy local cheeses here.

From the dairy farm continue towards 'L'Arpiha' on a wide track signposted 'Itinéraire'. When you come to a **clearing** at spot height 1648 m (**30min**), signs point straight ahead to L'Arpiha. But instead, take the fork *half-left* here. This shady and mostly

**Distance:** 9km/5.6mi; 2h40min
**Grade:** easy-moderate, with ascents/descents of about 280m/920ft; good tracks and paths. The scramble to the Arpiha summit demands some agility. Yellow PR waymarking. *IGN map 3741 ET*
**Equipment:** see page 9; sun protection (if only for sitting on the terrace at the Trois Vallées!)
**Transport:** 🚌 340/360 from Vauban to the Col de Turini (Mon/Wed/Thu *on demand*: tel 0800 060106 to arrange — it helps to speak French — no later than 4pm the day before you want to travel; journey 1h30min. Or 🚗 to the Col de Turini
**Refreshments:** cafés and restaurants at the Col de Turini
**Points of interest:**
Turini forest and pass
Authion Massif

grassy path undulates along the south side of the Scoubayoun ridge. Breaks in the trees afford glimpses down left over Turini and the hairpin road. Keep right uphill at a fork 15 minutes along (as waymarked).

At signpost 236 (**1h05min**), go straight ahead for 'L'Arpiha'. You come to a second signpost numbered 236 at a grassy **col**. From here scramble up to the **Cime de l'Arpiha** (1634m/5360ft; **1h25min**), to enjoy magnificent views — west to the deeply-

In the venerable forests of Turini, on the path to the Tête de Scoubayoun etched Planchette and Bollène valleys dropping to the Vésubie, and east to the spread of the Authion.*

Return to the *first 236 signpost you met on the way up* and turn left. This path rises 150m/495ft in deep shade to the highest point in the walk, the **Tête de Scoubayoun**, then drops 50m/ 165ft back to the clearing at spot height 1648 m. Turn left here, to retrace your steps back to the **Col de Turini (2h40min)**.

*A natural fortress because of its steep sides and strategic location on Italian border, the Authion has twice been the scene of bloody battles. Just after the birth of the French Republic, troops of the Austro-Sardinian coalition occupied the summit, and all Republican efforts to take it failed … until Napoleon took charge. Encircling the mountain with troops, he cut off the enemy's supply lines and won the County of Nice for the Republicans. In World War II the Authion was the last place in France to be liberated, only two weeks before the end of the war, after heavy bombardment and a battle lasting three days. *If you came by car, the circuit (signposted from the Col de Turini) round the Authion is a must!*

# Les Trois Vallées

The Col de Turini comes alive with the Monte Carlo Rally in January (when it must be deafening), but in early spring and autumn, when the area is at its best for walking, all is silence.

The col is served by a cluster of hotels, but the oldest — and our favourite — is the Trois Vallées. Although we haven't stayed

**LES TROIS VALLEES**
**Col de Turini** ( **04 93 04 23 23**
**www.les3vallees-turini.fr**
**open all year €-€€ (2 menus at 28 € and 33 €)**

standard four-course **regional menu** always available:

**entree:** plate of mountain ham/salad with mountain ham/*sanguin* mushrooms (photo page 125)/crêpe filled with goats' cheese and minced mushrooms

**mains:** venison stew/trout stuffed with *foie gras* and apples in Normandy sauce/veal fillet with *girolles* (wild mushrooms)

**interlude:** samples of 'shepherds' specialities'

**desserts:** myrtle or raspberry tarte, mixed ice creams/*crème brûlée* with lavender

overnight for a few years, no trip to Nice is complete without afternoon tea on their terrace — especially in September, when the rowans are weighed down with fat red berries.

Naturally you'll find hearty mountain cooking at all the Turini hotels. With luck there will be wild boar or venison on the menu. We don't remember exactly how the Trois Vallées did the memorable dish of venison with mushrooms that we so enjoyed several years ago, but opposite is a rather unusual French recipe for fruited venison — a change from the more common sauce flavoured with red currants.

restaurants

eat

# VENISON STEAKS WITH BLACKBERRIES

Gently cook the blackberries and sugar in a saucepan, stirring with a wooden spoon, until puréed. Add the vinegar, stock and cinnamon; bring to the boil, then simmer for 30min. Add the wine and cook for 5min more. Strain into another saucepan. Little by little, add 40 g of the butter, whisking all the time, and reduce until you have an fairly thick sauce. Season with salt and pepper to taste and keep warm.

In the rest of the butter (30 g), fry together the *lardons,* shallots and garlic. When they are golden, put in the mushrooms and cook for just a few minutes, then add the parsley. Set aside and keep warm.

In a heavy-bottomed frying pan, fry the venison in the olive oil as you like it (we think it's best a bit pink). Season, Then serve accompanied by the blackberry sauce and mushrooms. This recipe is ideal with potato cake (see page 60) — or even store-bought *rosti.*

Ingredients (for 4 people)

4 venison steaks *(pavé de biche)*
70 g butter, in small pieces
125 g bacon bits *(lardons)*
4 shallots, minced
50 ml red wine
400 ml stock
2 tbsp olive oil
100 g blackberries *(mûres)*
20 g caster sugar
1 tbsp red wine vinegar
1/2 cinnamon stick
400 g fresh *chanterelle* mushrooms (or *girolles*), sliced
2 cloves garlic, crushed
1 tbsp chopped parsley
salt and pepper to taste

recipes

eat

We've been exploring the south of France for many years, doing what we like most — walking, eating and sampling local wines. Before we started our own publishing company and had more leisure (and money!), our excursions were often based on the many châteaux-hotels in the area. We toured from place to place, stayed a night or two, with a good hike during the day and a 5-star meal in the evening.

In the 1990s John started with the first of his food intolerances, when he was diagnosed coeliac (no more *baguettes* for the lunchtime picnic during a hike, no more *croissants* with 'elevenses', no more *tarte aux pommes*)!

Some coeliacs become lactose intolerant over time; many other people are lactose intolerant without being coeliac. True lactose intolerance doesn't just mean avoiding cow's milk, etc, but *all* milks, butters, creams, yoghurts, and cheeses — whether from cows, goats or sheep. Another blow — no more *fromage*…

Food intolerances are becoming ever more recognised, and we know *there are a lot of you out there!* Even if you have learned to cope at home, it can be very daunting to go on holiday. *Will the food in restaurants be safe? Will I be able to buy gluten- and dairy-free foods?*

If you suffer a food intolerance you have probably already learned at home that what initially seems a penance in fact becomes a challenge and eventually a joy. We eat far healthier meals now than we did before, with fewer additives.

EAT GF, DF

Nowhere is this more enjoyable than in the south of France, where olive oil, fish, tomatoes and 'alternative' grains and flours are basic to the diet. Many, many dishes are *naturally* gluten- and dairy-free.

Of course food intolerances *are* restrictive — in the sense that we have to seek out or bake gluten-free breads and sweets, and we always need access to dairy-free 'milk', 'cream', 'yoghurt' and 'butter'. So over the years we've sussed out eating gf, df around the Med, and it's *so simple*.

# EATING IN RESTAURANTS

Many **entrées** are suitable, among them cold meat plates like the one on page 139. Bring your own bread! Salads are also common, just avoid those with goats' cheese. The ubiquitous brown fish soup *(soupe de poissons;* also sold in supermarkets) is also gf, df — just bring your own croutons!

For **main courses** one is spoilt for choice. If you're a sauce addict, like John, here's some very good news. Sauces are virtually *always* made by 'reduction' (cooked over a moderate heat until it becomes syrupy, as opposed to being thickened with wheat flour). But of course, you will *ask in advance* (see inside back cover). Many **steaks** are served in a mushroom and wine sauce — divine.

Anything '*à la provençale*' will be gf, df — generally this means with tomato, onion and garlic, as well as other spices and perhaps mushrooms, black olives and/or anchovies.

**Fish** dishes, unless grilled or poached, *may* well contain a least a dusting of flour, since fish is a bit difficult to fry

**135**

otherwise. *But not impossible.* If you ask, in a restaurant that *you trust*, they will do it without flour (or bring your own flour). Ask also if the sauce contains any cream or milk.

Give the **cheese course** a miss — unless, like John, you break out the 'lactase tablets' (now widely available at chemists and health food shops; just search the web) and treat yourself for a change. They really do work, and he uses them for special occasions (a magnificent cheese board) or when we share a 'full works' omelette (it is so much better with cheese) or some *moules farcies* in butter.

We are usually too full to have **dessert**, but some restaurants have chocolate sweets that are completely gf, df. Sorbets are also a good way to round off a meal … especially sorbets with liqueurs (our favourite is pear sorbet with *poire William*).

And as you may know already, *socca*, Nice's speciality snack, which makes a smashing lunch, is 100% gf, df.

# SELF-CATERING

While many hotels cater for food intolerances, we discovered the joy of self-catering — whether in a country cottage or an apart-hotel in the city — years ago. What a liberation! Room to swing a cat (or, more likely, chop up a rabbit). Tables where you can spread out your maps and bus timetables. Sofas to loll about on with a good book on a rainy day.

But for a special occasion, we might just book a night or two in one of the châteaux for old time's sake; it's relatively easy to cope for just a couple of nights. Then back to base with the laundry and gf bread waiting in the freezer.

## Gf, df shopping

The supermarkets these days are well stocked with gf products, as they are at home. But if we've not been able to get everything we need, there is a health food chain that can come to the rescue. It's called **Le Marchand Bio**, and the main branch in Nice centre is at 6 Rue Cassini (just below Galibaldi on the way to the port; 36 on the plan; ( 04 93 07 22 12). There's another, smaller branch at 2 Rue de la Buffa (just west of Place Grimaldi; 33 on the plan; ( 04 93 82 56 14).

Usually we can get everything we want on Rue Cassini, but there is a much larger branch just a short way out of the centre, on the 33 bus route to Mont Boron (Walk 1). Watch the names of the stops as the bus climbs the hill: pass Terra Amata and A de Joly; get off at the *next* stop, Pré Fossati. Then walk a short way down-

### GF, DF supermarket shopping

Our favourite supermarket chains, Casino and Intermarché, stock some very useful products:

Tournolive is top of the list — a dairy-free cooking/baking/spreading margarine, which tastes delicious and does *not* spit when used for frying

socca crisps — these are new (why didn't anyone think of this before?!)

soya/almond/coconut/rice milks and various natural or flavoured yoghurts

Camargue salt *(fleur de sel)*: this usually comes in such a lovely container with cork lid that it makes a great and inexpensive gift for those back home;

jams (Baptistin Feraud is particularly good;

gf, df tinned 'stews': Casino's own-brand *Saucisses aux lentilles à la graisse d'oil* or *Petit salé aux lentilles.* Mix either with a tin of chopped tomatoes and a glass of wine and *voilà*: dinner in a moment! (*Beware*: most other brands of these tinned stews are *not* gf, so read the label)

soupe de poissons à la provençale: this comes in a large glass jar and all hill, and the shop (10 Corniche André de Joly, ℂ 04 93 26 38 02) will be on your left, in a small shopping area. (There is also a large car park, if you are driving).

Some of the things to look out for at Le Marchard Bio are:

- simply delicious soya yoghurts. There is a great variety available in small sizes (150 g), in both glass jars and plastic containers;
- soya, almond, coconut or rice 'milks', if you haven't found them in the supermarket;
- soya 'cream' — a *must* for cooking. In France it is called Soya *Cuisine* (it's the same product that is available in the UK as Soya *Dream*);
- gluten-free breads: the widely-available Italian brands like Schär and Procelli are available in supermarkets, but look out too for Gerblé and other French bakers;
- gluten-free biscuits and cakes: here are some new brands to try: Lima, Biscuterie de Provence, Ikalia, Biscru, Le Pain des Fleurs, Nature & Compagnie;
- gluten-free flour: all kinds of gf flours are on sale — why not get some chick-pea flour to make *socca* at home (see recipe on page 30)? We love chestnut flour, too.
- Rapunzel 'Soma' dairy-free margarine made in Avignon; contains 50% sunflower oil and *doesn't spit* when frying — it's our favourite, but hard to find.

## Gf, df cooking

We've made all the **recipes** in this book using gluten- and dairy-free ingredients. Basically we just used a 1:1 substitution —

Gf dish at Balthazar (see page 103) — the beautiful large mixed platter. It can be df too — just a meat platter

remember, we are just amateur cooks — and the cooking method was unchanged. We've been more than happy with the results! The only cooking problem we have is with *frying,* when the recipe calls for a mixture of oil and butter (or just butter). Most vegetable fats spit all over the place. But Tournolive (from supermarkets) and Soma (from health food shops) are far better than any other 100% df spreads we've used because they contain *less water.*

## CONVERSION TABLES

| Weights | | Volume | | Oven temperatures | | |
|---|---|---|---|---|---|---|
| 10 g | 1/2 oz | 15 ml | 1 tbsp | | | gas |
| 25 g | 1 oz | 55 ml | 2 fl oz | °C | °F | mark |
| 50 g | 2 oz | 75 ml | 3 flz oz | 140°C | 275°F | 1 |
| 110 g | 4 oz | 150 ml | 1/4 pt | 150°C | 300°F | 2 |
| 200 g | 7 oz | 275 ml | 1/2 pt | 170°C | 325°F | 3 |
| 350 g | 12 oz | 570 ml | 1 pt | 180°C | 350°F | 4 |
| 450 g | 1 lb | 1 l | 1-3/4 pt | 190°C | 375°F | 5 |
| 700 g | 1 lb 8 oz | 1.5 l | 2-1/2 pt | 200°C | 400°F | 6 |
| 900 g | 2 lb | | | 220°C | 425°F | 7 |
| 1.35 g | 3 lb | | | 230°C | 430°F | 8 |
| | | | | 240°C | 475°F | 9 |

## MENU ITEMS

*à point* medium rare

*agneau* lamb

  *de lait* milk-fed

*agnelet* young lamb

*aïado* lamb with herbs and garlic

*aigre-doux* sweet and sour

*ail* garlic

*aïoli* mayonnaise with garlic (see p. 68-69)

*aligot* potato purée with cream, butter, garlic and fresh cheese

*aiglefin* haddock

*allumette* puff pastry

*amande* almond

*amer* bitter

*anchoïade* sauce of anchovies, olive oil and garlic

*anchois* anchovy

*andouille* smoked tripe sausage

*andouillette* small tripe sausage

*aneth* dill

*anis* aniseed

*arachide* peanut

*arête* fish bone (*sans arêtes* = filleted)

*aromates* aromatic spices

*artichaut* artichoke

*asperges* asparagus

*assiette de* plate of

*avocat* avocado

*basilic* basil

*beignet* fritter

*bleu* very rare

*biche* female deer

*blettes* Swiss chard

*boeuf* beef

*bourride* fish stew; see p. 68

*brandade de morue* salt cod

*brochette* skewered

*cabillaud* salt cod fritters

*caille* quail

*caillette* pork and vegetable faggot

*calamars* squid

*canard* duck

*caneton* duckling

*carré* cutlet or chop from best end of neck

*carvi* caraway

*céléri* celery

*céléri-rave* celeriac

*cèpes* ceps (delicate, highly-prized mushrooms)

*champignons* mushrooms

*de paris* button —

*chanterelles* golden-coloured mushrooms

*chevreau* kid

*chevreuil* roe-deer

*choix, au* choice of

*chou* cabbage

*chou-fleur* cauliflower

*confit* preserved

*coquillages* shellfish

*coquilles st-jacques* scallops

*côte* chop, side

*coulis* thick sauce

*courge* pumpkin

*crabe* crab

*crevettes*

  *grises* shrimp

  *roses* prawns

*crudités* raw vegetables

*daube* stew; see p. 102

*daurade/dorade* sea-bream

*dinde* young hen turkey

*dindon* turkey

*écrevisses* freshwater crayfish

*entrecôte* rib steak

*escabêche* marinated fish or poultry, served cold

*escargots* snails

*estouffade* beef stew with onions, herbs and red wine

*faisan* pheasant

*foie gras* goose liver

*fricandeau* slice of topside veal

*fritures* tiny fried fish

*fruits de mer* seafood

*gambas* giant prawns

*gibier* game

*gratiné* browned with butter and breadcrumbs

*grenadin* thick veal escalope

*grenouille* frog

  *cuisse de* — frogs' legs

*grillé* grilled

*farci* stuffed

*fleurs de courgettes* courgette flowers

*haricots* beans

  — *verts* green beans

*homard* lobster

*huîtres* oysters

*jambon* ham

  *fumé* smoked

# GLOSSARY

*langouste* spiny lobster
*langue* tongue
*lapereau* young rabbit
*lapin* rabbit
*légumes* vegetables
*lièvre* hare
  *civet de —* jugged hare
*longue* loin
*lotte (de mer)* monkfish
*loup (de mer)* sea-bass
*miel* honey
*mignon* small (round) piece
*morue* cod
*moules* mussels
*noix* nuts
*oignon* onion
*pain/pan* bread
  *bagnat* thick sandwich; see p. 28
*pâtes* pasta
*pané* with breadcrumbs
*panisses* chick-pea fritters
*persil* parsley
*persillade* chopped parsley and garlic
*petit* small
*pignons* pine nuts
*pissaladière* pizza; see p. 28
*pistou* mixture of garlic, basil, tomatoes and olive oil, blended

with mortar and pestle
*poire* pear
*poireau* leek
*poisson* fish
*poivron* sweet pepper
*potage* thick soup
*poussin* baby chicken
*Provençale, à la* with tomatoes, olive oil, garlic
*raisins* grapes
*rascasse* scorpion fish
*ravigote* sauce with onions, herbs, mushrooms, wine vinegar
*rémoulade* sauce with mayonnaise, mustard, capers, anchovies, herbs
*rognons* kidneys
*rouget* red mullet
*rouille* mayonnaise-like sauce with peppers, garlic and saffron
*safran* saffron
*salade Niçoise* salad with tuna, tomatoes, anchovies, hard-boiled egg, black olives
*sanglier* wild boar
*sarriette* savoury, bitter herb
*socca* 'pancake' made with chick-

pea flour; see p. 28
*saumon* salmon
*sole* sole
*suprême* boneless breast
*tapenade* paste of black olives, anchovies and capers (called 'Provençal caviar')
*tarte* open pastry case
*telline* small clam
*terrine* cold 'loaf' of fish, meat or pâté (named for the container in which it is cooked)
*tourte* sweet-filled pastry case, pie
*de blettes* chard pie (see p. 127)
*truccha* Nice-style omelette with Swiss chard or wild asparagus and garlic
*truite* trout
*turbot/turbotin* turbot
*velouté* white sauce
*veau* veal
*volaille* poultry

**SHOPPING TERMS**

anchovies *anchois*
apple *pomme*
artichoke *artichaut*
asparagus *asperges*

avocado *avocat*
bacon bits (*lardons*)
  unsmoked (*lardons nature*)
bass, sea *loup de mer*
bay leaf *laurier*
beans *haricots*
  green *haricots verts*
**beef *boeuf* cuts:**
  boneless *sans os*
  fillet *filet*
  flank *bavette*
  fore rib *entrecôte*
  rib *côte*
  rump *rumsteak*
  shin *jarret*
  shoulder *paleron*
  sirloin *contrefilet*
  strip loin *faux-filet*
  tongue *langue*
beer *bière*
blackberries *mûres*
brandy *cognac*
bread *pain*
bream, sea *daurade*
butter *beurre*
cake *gâteau*
caraway *carvi*
carrot *carotte*
celeriac *céléri-rave*
celery *céléri*
chard, Swiss *blettes*
cheese *fromage*
cherries *cerises*
chestnuts, sweet *châtaignes*
chicken *poulet*
  baby *poussin*
chocolate *chocolat*

141

cider *cidre*
cloves *girofles*
cod *morue*
coffee *café*
condiments *condiments*
corn
  meal *farine de maïs*
  starch *amidon de maïs*
courgettes *courgettes*
crab *crabe*
crayfish *écrevisses*
cream *crème*
cucumber *concombre*
duck *canard*
  preserved *confit*
eggs *oeufs*
fennel *fenouil*
fish *poisson*
flour (wheat) *farine*
  chick-pea *farine de pois chiches*
  corn *farine de maïs*
fruit *fruit*
game *gibier*
garlic *ail*
goose *oie*
  grease *graisse d'oie*
  liver *foie gras*
grapes *raisins*
haddock *aiglefin*
ham *jambon*
  smoked *fumé*
hare *lièvre*
herbs *herbes*
ice cream *glace*

juice *jus*
juniper *genièvre*
**lamb *agneau***
milk-fed *agneau de lait*
  **cuts:**
  boneless *sans os*
  cutlets from best end of neck *carré*
  leg (including chump) *gigot*
  loin *filet*
  shouler *épaule*
leek *poireau*
lemon *citron*
lettuce *laitue*
liver *foie*
lobster *homard*
  spiny *langouste*
milk *lait*
monkfish *lotte de mer*
mullet, red *rouget*
mushrooms *champignons*
mussels *moules*
mustard *moutarde*
nuts *noix*
  peanuts *arachides*
olive oil *huile d'olive*
onions *oignons*
oysters *huîtres*
parsley *persil*
pasta *pâtes*
pastry *pâtisserie*
pear *poire*
peas *pois/petits pois*
pepper (spice) *poivre*
pepper (sweet) *poivron*

pheasant *faisan*
pine nuts *pignons*
**pork *porc***
rind *couennes*
  **cuts:**
  boneless *sans os*
  chop *côte*
  cutlet from best end of neck *carré*
  escalope *escalope*
  fillet *filet*
  loin *longue*
potatoes *pommes de terre*
poultry *volaille*
prawns *crevettes*
  giant *gambas*
pumpkin *courge*
quail *caille*
rabbit *lapin*
  young *lapereau*
raspberries *framboises*
rice *riz*
rosemary *romarin*
saffron *safran*
salmon *saumon*
salt *sel*
  sea *(fleur de sel)*
sausage
  fresh *saucisse*
  dry *saucisson*
scallops *coquilles (St-Jacques)*
scorpion fish *rascasse*
shallots *echalotes*
shellfish *coquillages*
shrimp *crevettes grises*
snails *escargots*

sole *sole*
soup *soupe*
soya *soja*
spices *épices*
spinach *épinards*
sugar *sucre*
tarragon *estragon*
tea *thé*
thyme *thym*
tomatoes *tomates*
trout *truite*
tuna *thun*
turbot *turbot, turbotin*
turkey *dindon*
  young *dinde*
**veal *veau***
  **cuts:**
  boneless *sans os*
  chop *côte*
  fillet *filet*
  kidneys *rognons*
  liver *foie*
  loin *carré*
  shin, knuckle *jarret*
  shoulder *épaule*
  sweetbreads *ris*
  topside *noix*
vegetables *légumes*
venison steaks *pavé de biche*
vinegar *vinaigre*
  wine *de vin*
water *eau*
  still *sans gaz*
  sparkling *avec gaz*
watercress *cresson*
wine *vin*
  dry *sec*
  red *rouge*
  white *blanc*

**bold type:** photograph; *italic type:* map

INDEX

walk & eat around NICE

Sixth edition © 2020
Published by Sunflower Books
PO Box 36061, London SW7 3WS
www.sunflowerbooks.co.uk

All rights reserved. No part of this publication may be reproduced, stored in a
retrieval system, or transmitted by any form or by any means, electronic,
mechanical, photocopying, recording or otherwise, without the prior written
permission of the publishers.

ISBN 978-1-85691-532-8

Cover photograph: Beaulieu and the hills of Walk 6 from Cap Ferrat (Walk 4)

Photographs: John Underwood, with the exception of pages 28, 29, 31, 41, 42,
    49, 49, 91, 92, 133 and the cover (Shutterstock)
Maps: Sunflower Books
Cookery editor: Marina Bayliss
Series designed by Jocelyn Lucas
A CIP catalogue record for this book is available from the British Library.
Printed and bound in England: Short Run Press, Exeter

**Before you go ...**
log on to
**www.sunflowerbooks.co.uk**
and click on '**updates**', to see if we have been notified of any changes to
the routes or restaurants.

**When you return ...**
do let us know if any routes have changed because of road-building, storm
damage or the like. Have any of our restaurants closed — or any new ones
opened *on the route of the walk?* (Not Nice restaurants, please; these books
are not intended to be complete restaurant guides!)

Send your comments to mail@sunflowerbooks.co.uk